LET THERE BE LIGHT

·1868·

This book was made possible through
the generous assistance of:

digital
Digital Equipment Corporation

FLUOR CORPORATION

IBM

Copyright © 1992 Collins Publishers San Francisco
All rights reserved, including the right of reproduction in
whole or in part in any form.

Library of Congress Cataloging-in-Publication Data:
MacNamara, Mark.
    In pursuit of ideas : a year in the life of the
University of California.
    p.   cm.
    Text by Mark MacNamara and Bernard Ohanian; photo-
graphs by Chris Maynard and others.
    ISBN 0-00-255005-9
    1. University of California (System) 2. University of
California (System)—Pictorial works. I. Ohanian, Bernard,
date. II. Maynard, Chris, date. III. Collins Publishers San
Francisco. IV. Title.
LD7298.M33 1992   92-517

Preceding page: Photograph by Chris Maynard
This page: Photograph by Ben Ailes
Printed and bound in Japan by Dai Nippon Printing Co., Ltd.
First printing July 1992
10 9 8 7 6 5 4 3 2 1

In Pursuit of Ideas

A Year in the Life of the University of California

Essays by Mark MacNamara

Collins Publishers San Francisco

A Division of HarperCollins*Publishers*

C alifornia was a raw frontier society, far removed from the centers of power, of influence, of culture, when its citizens determined to create a university. The University of California, chartered in 1868, opened with one campus in Oakland, and from that small seed its fruits have spread across the state, the nation and the world. Compared to many of the great universities of the world, the University of California, which is celebrating its 125th birthday, is an adolescent. Yet in a relatively short lifetime, it has become the premier public university in the United States and earned a place among the most distinguished institutions of learning anywhere.

The University of California now comprises nine campuses, five teaching hospitals, more than 200 laboratories and research centers, more than 100 libraries and an impressive array of teaching, research and public-service programs. More than a quarter of a million people attend the university as students or work for it as faculty, administrators and staff. Research ships from the Scripps Institution of Oceanography explore the world's oceans; astronomers at the Keck Observatory operate the world's largest telescope; archeologists uncover the past, layer by fascinating layer, during excavations in ancient lands. UC carries out roughly 11 percent of the basic research funded by the federal government that is conducted in our nation's universities. It graduates about 10 percent of all Ph.D.s in the United States every year, and more women and minority Ph.D.s than any other university. Its faculty includes more than 250 members of the National Academy of Sciences, about one-sixth of the total membership. Through the years, 29 UC faculty members have won Nobel prizes, and 18 of those laureates remain active on the faculty.

Whether they know it or not, the people of California are touched by their university every day. UC-trained architects and engineers design the buildings we live in and the roads we travel. Graduates of the schools and colleges in the health sciences care for us when we are ill and discover the miracle drugs that give us hope in the fight against disease. UC's faculty educates talented young people in the high standards of commitment and performance essential to the quality of all the professions, from architecture to law. California's oldest industry—agriculture—has been revolutionized and its youngest—biotechnology—virtually created by researchers at the University of California.

Jim Gensheimer

The university has been called the state's crowning jewel, and with good reason: it is the principal point of access for people of talent and ambition, a quiet force from which much of California's economic power and strength derive, one of the world's great intellectual treasure houses, the repository of much of our cultural heritage, a cauldron of discovery, a marketplace of ideas—in short, one of the greatest centers of learning the world has ever known.

It is not easy to reflect the astonishing breadth and depth of such a place, but this extraordinary book succeeds. Its magnificent photographs capture the daily pulse of a great university: bright, eager undergraduates stimulated by their first exposure to scholarship; determined graduate and professional students embarking on the rigors of intellectual appren-

Mark Wexler

ticeship; scholars at the cutting edge of 21st-century knowledge; administrators and staff dedicated to creating an environment in which teaching, research and public service flourish.

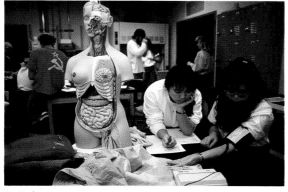
Jim Gensheimer

This book is a tribute to the University of California, and thus it is also a tribute to the Californians who, from 1868 to this very day, have supported their university and helped make it a paradigm of public higher education. It is being published as I step down as president. The distinguished head of UC's Irvine campus, Chancellor Jack W. Peltason, succeeds me as the university's 16th president. This book is a visual expression of the trust that is collectively the University of California and which now passes from one administration to another.

I am delighted that Collins Publishers has found in UC such extensive opportunities for visual and literary exploration, and I salute the photographers, designers, writers, and editors for producing a truly memorable work for the benefit of all who value the contributions and achievements of colleges and universities everywhere.

Chris Maynard

David Pierpont Gardner

Stockbroker and UCLA alumnus Geoffrey Strand leads football fans in cheers as the Bruins play the University of Oregon Ducks. *Photographer: Mark Wexler*

Throughout the university, it's easy to find evidence of calculating minds at work. *Photographer: Andy Levin*

Students at UC Santa Cruz form the chorus for a contemporary Balinese music and dance piece known as a *kecak*.
Photographer: Jim Gensheimer

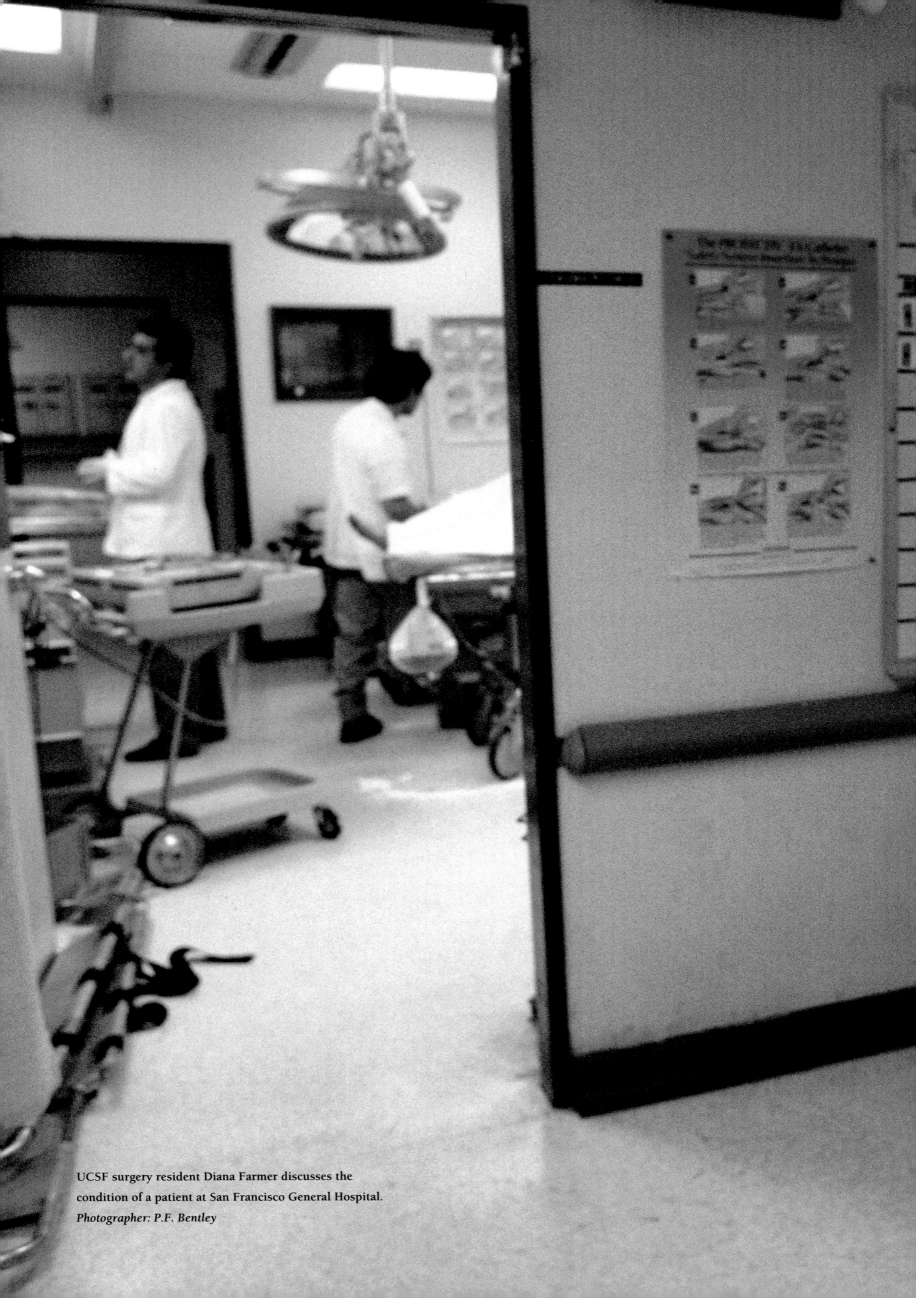

UCSF surgery resident Diana Farmer discusses the
condition of a patient at San Francisco General Hospital.
Photographer: P.F. Bentley

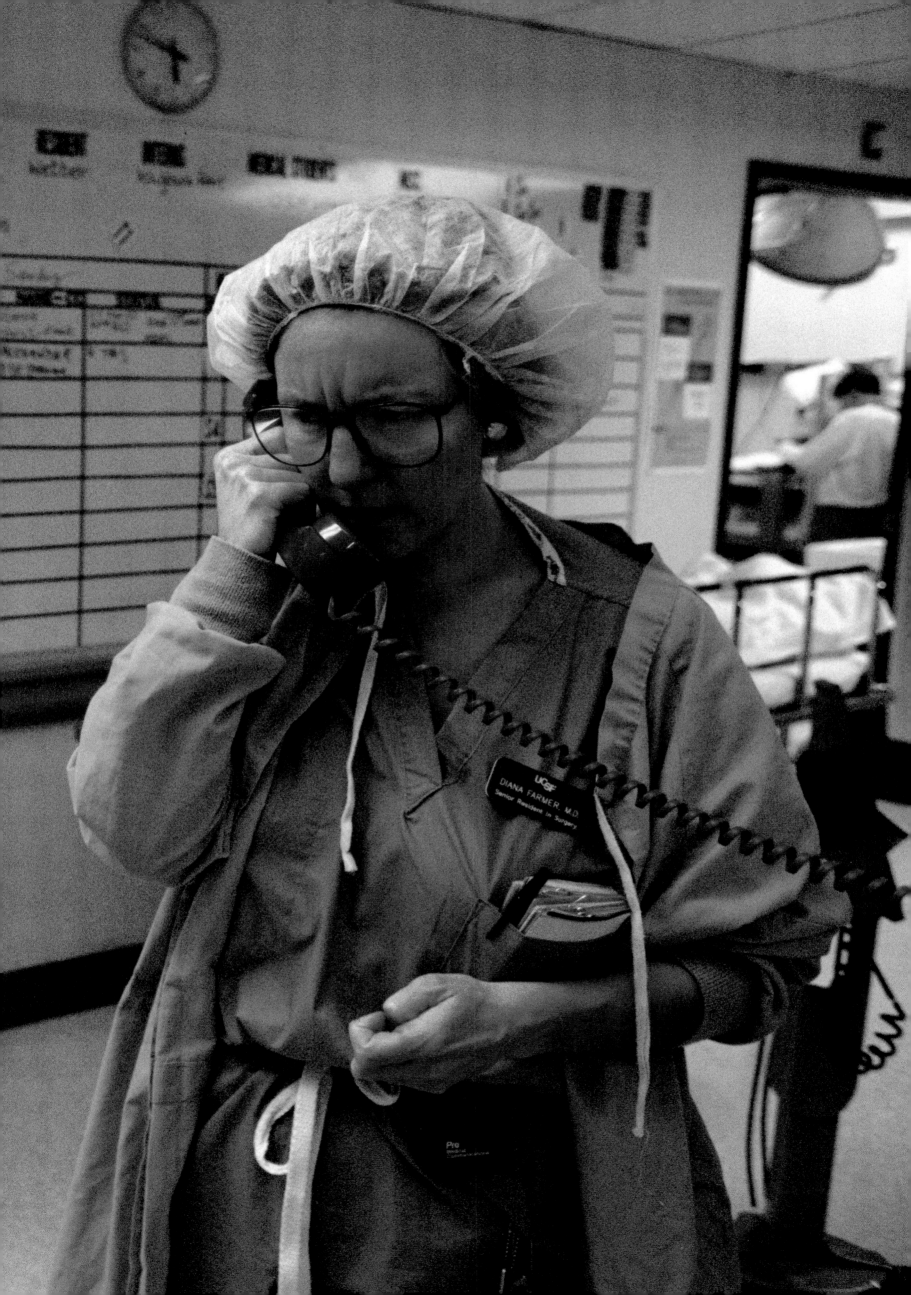

Finished with classes for the day, students at UCLA head for home. *Photographer: Ricardo DeAratanha*

The cameras are out; the Kleenex will soon follow. Graduates from UC San Diego file past family and friends. *Photographer: Rick Rickman*

THE PROMISE IN THE ROCK

Berkeley

Davis

Irvine

Los Angeles

Riverside

San Diego

San Francisco

Santa Barbara

Santa Cruz

No one knew of Founders' Rock. "Sorry, I've only been here one semester," said a young Asian woman. "I'm not familiar with that." "Don't know it," said a student in a CAL sweatshirt. "Maybe over near the Campanile." Nearer the Campanile, and still no one knew. Finally, a young man in wire-rimmed glasses stopped: "Yes, just follow that path. You want to get to the northeast corner of the campus. That way."

The path struck off from the Campanile, the 307-foot bell tower that stands like the gnomon of an enormous sundial in the midst of the Berkeley campus. Two hundred yards away, beyond the Hearst Memorial Mining Building and just behind the electron microscope facility, at the corner of Hearst Street and Gayle Road, there was an outcropping of rock. The rock was shaped in such a way that one homeless person could find half a shelter underneath and, judging by a piece of burned wood and an empty sardine can, someone had been there recently. It was an ironic commentary: Founders' Rock, symbol of a great institution whose original charter was "promotion of the highest welfare of the state." And Founders' Rock, reminder of promises to keep.

The "main" entrance is from the Hearst Street side. There's a dog path leading off the sidewalk up five yards to the spot, and there, embedded in the rock, among ferns and moss, is a California marble plaque not much bigger than an old-fashioned Oxford Dictionary, bearing the words "College of California, April 16, 1860. Inscribed May 9, 1896."

It is an immodestly modest marker of what has become one of the most powerful *systems* of university education in the world—powerful not in terms of reputation or the pervasiveness and depth of its influence throughout California's infrastructure, though that's substantial, or even in terms of the specific contributions which outstanding graduates and professors have made to the arts and sciences, and to government. That all seems incidental compared with the system's sheer wealth of knowledge, and its ability to transmit that knowledge to the world.

Consider the energy to be tapped: more than 125,000 undergraduates culled from the top 12.5 percent of the state's high-school reservoir; 40,000 graduate students; 7,500 faculty members—including 18 Nobel prize winners, second only in number to Harvard. And then add the many multicultural infusions; 20 million library books; 150 associated research institutes, laboratories, extension centers and field stations. And tradition itself, borne far and wide by 800,000 living alumni. In sum, a vast hot pot of brains and cultures, personal experience, dreams and ambition—and varying amounts of moral purpose—all gurgling up beneath a state which has become the sixth largest economy in the world; the synapse point between North and South America and the Pacific Rim; and a nation within a nation, with all the problems and potential solutions that the western world is likely to face in the first half of the 21st century.

Meanwhile, back on the path that runs by Founders' Rock, eight out of ten students had no idea where the rock was. One of the two people who did know, a junior, had no thought as to what significance the rock might have. The other was Joe Orr, a research assistant specializing in lipoprotein research in the physics department. "That's it, right over your shoulder," he said with a wry smile, and he went on to tell of the rock's recent mythology. About the people seen near it, including a long-haired young man who some years ago sat atop the rock for several days—whether stoned, enduring personal tragedy or contemplating the Dancing Wu-Li Masters, Orr didn't know.

"There are a few stories like that," he said, and he mentioned some other historical points at Berkeley: Sather Gate; South Hall; once upon a time, the Wheeler Oak; various benches; and of course the Campanile. "But you know, if you want to find out about mythology, go to the Lawrence Laboratory, the old Rad Lab, see the Cyclotron. The real mythology here is in the sciences."

LEFT: UC Berkeley's main library, named after turn-of-the-century philanthropist Charles Franklin Doe, offers anthropology student Simone Katz a quiet corner in the sun. The largest of the 24 libraries on the Cal campus, Doe houses about half of the school's 7 million volumes. *Photographer: Chris Maynard*

The people who put UC on the map came mostly from Yale University. They were Congregationalists (now the United Church of Christ): Calvinists, whose great-grandfathers had been thrown out of England and Holland in the late 1500s, then made their way to New Haven. They landed with an orthodox tradition that had no use for popes, bishops, statues or ceremonies. Mass was celebrated with grape juice, not wine. Thanksgiving and Christmas were not celebrated at all. Altogether, folks not easily intimidated, and with a strong idea that a university should serve both church and state. The Yale men arrived in northern California in 1849. The state was gold crazy. Land owners had lost their laborers to the mines. A system of higher education was needed to root the place.

Riverside

"Individuality is carried to an extreme in California," wrote the Rev. Henry Durant, who in 1870 became UC's first president. "Our fast living may almost all of it be referred to intense selfishness. Indeed, sentimentality and idealism seem lost from the mass of people. They are sensualists and materialists, or nearer that than anything else—the very condition on account of which the Spirit of God forsook the antediluvian world."

Naturally, the Congregationalists were swallowed up by the place they came to tame. The need of those who wanted a university was less to serve the

Santa Barbara

church or to understand the despair of King Ozymandius than to engineer, to build, to grow a great seed, and make the soil a servant. Although he envisioned a comprehensive liberal arts education, it was miners, engineers and farmers that University of California president Daniel Gilman had foremost in his mind when he spoke in 1872 at the university's first inaugural address:

"Science is the mother of California. Give us more and not less science; encourage the most thorough and prolonged search for the truth which is to be found in the rocks, the sea, the oil, the air, the sun and stars; in light and heat and magnetic forces; in plants and animals and in the human frame; but let us also learn the lessons which are embodied in language and literature, in laws and institutions, in doctrines and opinions, in historical progress ..."

The Lawrence Berkeley Laboratory stands high in the hills above the campus. On clear days, particularly at sunset, the view of the Bay, San Francisco and the Pacific Ocean beyond offers a special magnificence—as though one were watching the edge of the world, and were at the center of it at the same time. In the 1920s and '30s (and for a while in the late 1940s), Lawrence Berkeley Laboratory *was* the center of the world. There were other science centers—at the University of Chicago, Harvard, Cal Tech and Princeton, not to mention Cavendish Laboratory at Cambridge and

Davis

the University of Göttingen in Germany—but for a long moment Berkeley was the leading school of theoretical physics, the center of the center. "California is the only university at which men refuse offers from Harvard," as one physicist put it at the time.

And so it was that the science giants of the day—physicists, chemists, biochemists, biologists, mathematicians and medical men—all joined together in an unusual collaboration and created the atomic world. And in creating this new world they helped create the fundamental mythology of our age. It was Ernest

Irvine; All photographs by Marcia Lippman

Lawrence who arranged it—another Yale man. He was King Arthur; the Radiation Laboratory, the Rad Lab, his court; first the Cyclotron, then ever bigger accelerators, his round table; science his Guinevere; and genius his Excalibur. And perhaps Robert Oppenheimer was his Sir Lancelot.

In the beginning, in the late 1920s, when Lawrence first arrived as a professor, there was a certain innocence among the men, and eventually the few women, who worked in the Rad Lab. All quicksilver minds, they came for the love of adventure and

San Francisco

exploration. The immediate object was to devise a "proton merry-go-round accelerator" that became known as the Cyclotron. Lawrence himself was legend almost from the beginning. His intelligence was matched with intuition, enormous self-confidence and an ability to guide people rather than push them. He worked alongside rather than from above. He solved problems himself, took care of his own. He made nearly all those in the Lab share in his devotion—his obsession—to Science. He was also the first professor from the University of California, indeed any state university, to win a Nobel prize.

The lab motto, taken from Lawrence, was "Start out and invent around the difficulties." There was little structure, no hierarchy—an elite club and yet with a strong aversion to snobbery. Competition and secrecy were frowned upon. Independence was paramount. Above all, the ethics were honesty and hard work—and ever more hard work. Exhaustion was common. Once a physicist worked until he literally collapsed from a nearly ruptured appendix. People often worked for no pay, just for the chance to play with the "Maestro."

Los Angeles

Glenn Seaborg, who later won the Nobel prize in chemistry for his work in discovering plutonium, became chancellor at Berkeley, and served as chairman of the Atomic Energy Commission, started out as a graduate student in the Rad Lab. "It was an extraordinary climate in the 1930s," he remembers, "and it was marked by much greater trust and freedom than you find today. For example, in the chemistry department, grad students were given keys to the storeroom; you could get whatever you needed.

"I walked in, a UCLA graduate, into this wonder world. The people I would see were all famous: Lawrence, Oppenheimer, Gilbert Newton Lewis, the greatest physical chemist in the world. And there were others whose names I'd seen in my textbooks for years: Joel Hildebrand, Wendell Latimer, William Bray. And they were all very open. It was always a team kind of effort."

After the war, King Arthur's court changed. Innocence was lost. There were splits. "Pure science" became public property. The commercialization of science became an issue. And then there were the Oppenheimer hearings in 1954, in which national and personal loyalties were tested in the accelerator of public opinion, and fear. The original romance dissipated, and Lawrence died in 1958.

C arl Jung had the notion that myths are metaphors for psychological transformation. A hero must endure peril. Peril is the cleansing process by which purity is revealed and from which, in Western culture, comes the knowledge and courage to find the holy grail. Such is the lesson that myths offer the hero in us all. As Joseph Campbell put it, "The first and most essential service of a mythology is of opening the mind and heart to the utter wonder of all being." Certainly that's the hope of any university, which is at once a repository and a generator of myths and folklore. At the University of California as elsewhere, each campus, each college, has its legends, its monsters and heroes.

San Diego

But there is something else here, which has to do with the nature of California. What an odd place! Forever tanning in its newness. Disparate, unstable, nervous and laid-back at the same time. Reverberating. Land of "strange attractors," as the Santa Cruzians, the UC physicists who began the study of chaos in the late 1970s, might describe it. California is the place where the traditions people bring with them eventually get tossed or sold, or more likely forgotten. It's the land of little or no inhibitions, where fact and fiction, present and future, credo and creativity all come together—opposing ideas often mixed together so that nothing is clear, nothing is sacred, but anything appears possible. It's that muck and promise that the University of California reflects—the illusion of freedom, of limitlessness, and the gift of optimism. That's the state, and the magic in Founders' Rock.

Santa Cruz

RIGHT: Looking for a little divine intervention never hurts—especially during a final exam in Human Parasitology, one of several options for fulfilling an important requirement for biological sciences majors at UC Irvine. Although the Orange County campus, which opened its doors in 1965, is perhaps best known for its programs in the physical and biological sciences, three-quarters of the 38 undergraduate degree programs offered by UCI are actually in the humanities, the fine arts and the social sciences.
Photographer: Jim Mendenhall

Above: Today's campus is a study in fashion, with everything from ties to T-shirts making the grade. Even in the days of the dress code, abolished in 1966, the style here at UC Davis, in the words of professor emeritus Charles Rick, was "delightfully informal compared to the Eastern schools." First-year students four decades ago might not have agreed: For years they were required to wear blue caps—with Cal Aggie emblazoned on them in gold lettering—to all classes until Homecoming Weekend. The caps, known as dinks, replaced a tradition in which first-year students wore bibs to signal their class affiliation. *Photographer: Annie Griffiths Belt*

Right: Intent on calculating the surface tension resulting from the flow of fluids through various-sized tubes, Aaron Romanowsky uses the tools at hand in professor Paul Hansma's physics class at Santa Barbara's College of Creative Studies. Unlike the more traditional approach to physics followed on other UC campuses, as well as in Santa Barbara's own College of Letters and Science, there are no lab procedures spelled out for science students at the College of Creative Studies: Professors present the problems and ask the students to come up with their own methods for solving them. About 150 undergraduates pursue UCSB degrees in art, biology, chemistry, literature, math, music composition and physics at the selective school-within-a-school. *Photographer: Andy Levin*

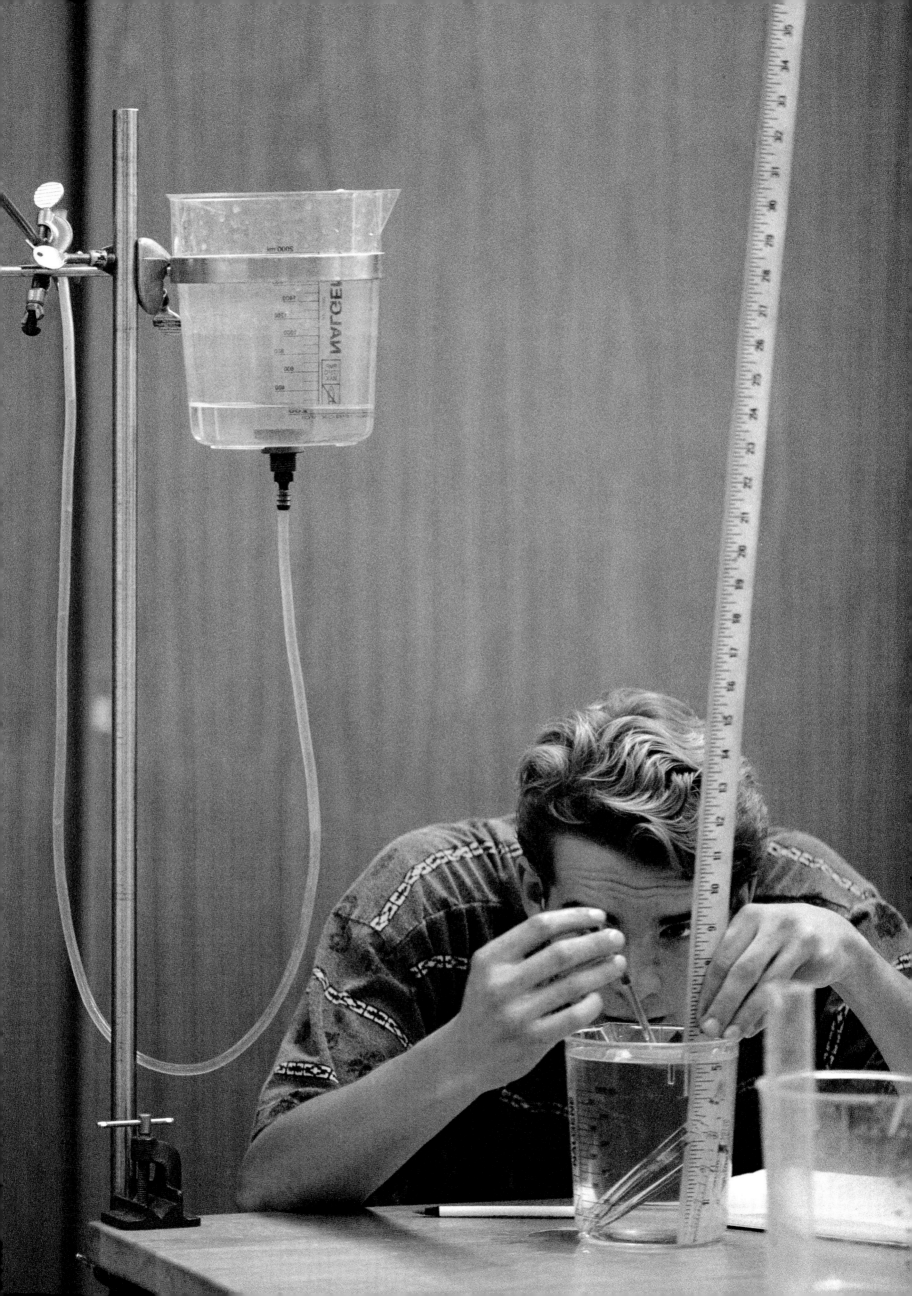

ABOVE: Alex Saragoza, associate professor of Chicano Studies, delivers a lecture to the hundreds of students enrolled in his Comparative Study of Immigration course at Berkeley. Incoming students at Cal are now required to take at least one course that addresses "theoretical and analytical issues relevant to understanding race, culture, and ethnicity in American history and society"—part of the university's effort to wrestle with the task of educating students in a state that is increasingly multiracial and multicultural. *Photographer: Andy Levin*

RIGHT: With one faculty member for every 18 students system-wide at UC, many classes at the nine campuses consist of intimate discussion groups. But Santa Barbara religious studies professor Walter Capps regularly packs 900 students into his course on the Vietnam War, and he turns away hundreds more. The students in the Campbell Hall auditorium—many of whom have parents who either fought in the war or were active in demonstrations against it—examine the war's impact on American values through the perspectives of guest lecturers ranging from former combat soldiers and POWs to war protestors and conscientious objectors. *Photographer: Dana Fineman*

RIGHT: Chris Fraser catches up on some physics in the library at Stevenson College, one of eight residential colleges at UC Santa Cruz. The emphasis at UCSC has been on undergraduate education since the doors first opened in 1965: Ninety percent of the campus's 10,000 students, in fact, are undergrads. Santa Cruz students affiliate with a college—Stevenson, Cowell, Crown, Merrill, Porter, Kresge, Oakes, or Eight—upon entering the university, based on the college's area of emphasis. They remain free, however, to take classes offered at any one of the colleges on the picturesque 2,000-acre campus. *Photographer: Jim Gensheimer*

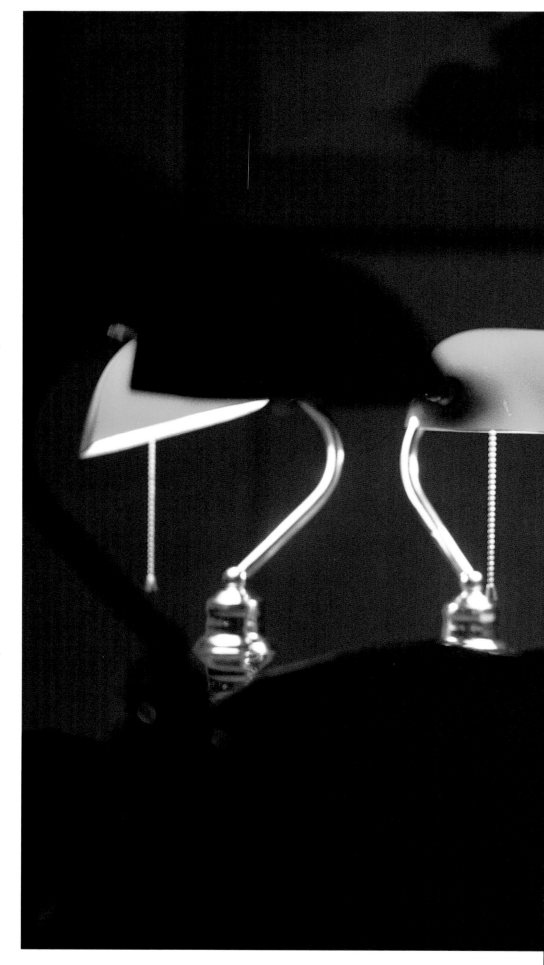

Left: If, as the 19th-century English biologist Thomas Huxley wrote, "the chess board is the world [and] the pieces the phenomena of the universe," then members of the chess club at Berkeley get quite a cosmic education during their monthly tournaments in and around Sproul Plaza. About 30 students belong to the chess club, which brought home the Pan-American Collegiate Chess Tournament Championship in 1989. The club is also fertile ground for employment recruiters, who seek out chess players because, says club president Peter Yu, "We've demonstrated our ability to think many moves ahead." Yu says he loves the game—which originated in the Indus Valley of India in the sixth century A.D.— because "it's very fair, and it engulfs your whole being." *Photographer: Ben Ailes*

Above: When the library's too crowded, there's always an alternative at UC Santa Barbara, where the beach is so close that the sound of crashing waves can be heard from some classrooms. Studying in the sand must be effective: More than 60 percent of UCSB's students go on to graduate school, and two-thirds of the graduates who apply to medical school are accepted. *Photographer: Jim Mendenhall*

ABOVE: Taking literally the mission of Santa Cruz's Porter College—"to apply the creative process to all fields"—Lisa Catterall and Susan Willowsong Nelson make a campus meadow their stage for a twilight dance to autumn's shortening days.
Photographer: Jim Gensheimer

RIGHT: Moments before taking to the water of the Oakland Estuary for a race against UCLA, members of Berkeley's women's varsity crew team talk strategy in the boat-house attic. Undeterred by practice sessions at dawn, more than 100 Cal students take part in the sport each year. Recognizing that interest, the Cal athletic department is the only one in the UC system to elevate crew above a club sport by paying for travel, equipment and staff salaries. Cal's tradition in crew compares favorably with that of the Ivy League schools: Three Golden Bears have gone on to win Olympic gold medals in crew, and rare is the U.S. Olympic crew team without at least one Berkeley athlete. *Photographer: Doug Menuez*

OVERLEAF: The serenity of a late fall afternoon is accentuated by the absence of cars at UC Davis, where the atmosphere evokes the small-town feel of rural Eastern schools rather than the big-city buzz of UCLA or Berkeley. Automobiles are banned from the central campus area, and most of the 22,000 students use bicycles to get around.

Photographer: Annie Griffiths Belt

One of the cruelest illusions of life at the end of the 20th century is that we know a great deal—about ourselves, about the earth, about our environment. The paradox is that we know so much and so little at the same time. Our knowledge seems great because it's always expanding, because it's all we know, and because we know so much more than the people before us. With some exceptions, perhaps, we know everything that has ever been known by people on earth.

Yet, always the paradox: we know we can play golf on the moon and breed sheep with horns, but we can barely predict the weather. We know we can get a damn good TV picture of Saturn's rings, we're facile with a space shuttle, we can make a mechanical heart—but we know little about the earth's core, or about the gases that once upon a time poured up out of the earth and which, some believe, created water, harboring life that eventually became human.

We believe in the theory of relativity, in the idea of a "mind," perhaps even a soul. We don't really believe in the Easter Bunny or magicians. We know the nature of tricks, yet as a society we're not all agreed whether Eve descended from an ape, or whether she was a pre-Raphaelite beauty sprung from the rib of Adam. Belief is an important aspect of our knowledge. Often we confuse what we know with what we believe we know. The curious thing is how little we know, how little we can say with certainty about where we came from.

For example, we don't even know why our civilization began where it did—in that sacred little crescent between the Tigris and Euphrates rivers. And we don't know why it began when it did—around 16,000 years ago. After all, our civilization might just as well have begun in the Nile Delta a few hundred miles to the west. Or along the west coast of North America, for that matter.

Actually, there's a new theory to explain Mesopotamia. It comes from Dr. James Kennett, a paleontologist at UC Santa Barbara who has an expertise in the extinction of some ocean fauna. For several years he studied environmental changes that might have led to the extinction of certain Cretaceous organisms in Antarctic waters at the start of the Paleocene epoch, about 57 million years ago. He concluded that global warming may have been associated with this particular extinction. He also concluded that even a brief occurrence of global warming (on the order of, say, 1,000 years) can "trigger a major threshold event, which in turn can have a large-scale environmental effect that can lead to the extinction of a species."

Dr. Kennett's theory about Mesopotamia is this: Since the last glaciation 18,000–20,000 years ago, sea levels have been rising. They're up about 360 feet. Between 14,000 and 6,000 years ago, the oceans rose very quickly. The ice sheets seem to have melted at a particularly high rate, though we don't know why. The water rose high enough to flood the arid lands beneath what we now call the Persian Gulf. Until then, that area was more or less desert. It had been made habitable by the fertility around the Tigris and Euphrates rivers, which ran through the Straits of Hormuz and formed an enormous delta out in the Indian Ocean, off what is now Oman.

So the water rises and gradually fills up the gulf. The hunters and gatherers who had made such a good living from game and berries are forced to retreat—albeit over the course of many centuries—as the estuaries recede to the northwest. But as resources contract, people begin to fight each other. Conflict spreads, and the first villages form—partly as a means of defense, and partly to allow people with different skills to live together. No longer are there just hunters and gatherers, but also weapons designers and manufacturers, construction workers, food preparation technicians, waste management types and so on. The villages expand until eventually the first cities appear at Eridu, Ur, Uruk and Lagash.

LEFT: Future marine biologist Alisha Griffin gets up-close and personal with a California sea lion—*Zalophus californianus*, if you please—at UC Santa Cruz's Long Marine Lab. Nearly 40,000 people visit the lab each year, including many scientists who come to utilize the specially equipped marine-mammal pools. *Photographer: Jim Gensheimer*

It took about 2,500 years for the Persian Gulf to fill up, from 9,000 to 6,500 years ago. In other words, it was just in those two-and-a-half millennia, unfindable seconds in the great wilderness of time, that humankind became "civilized."

Dr. Kennett's theory has broad significance in terms of the environment. "This is an example," he says, "of how much we are slaves of the environment, and how much we need to be aware of its effect. As a modern example, I think of Southern California, which is so dependent upon [imported] water. This is particularly true in Santa Barbara, where the water crisis has led to an enormous conflict over how to respond and what to do about the future. It is the confluence of population and resources, and how our environment affects these resources, which is the most important issue facing the world today."

The problem with trying to understand the environment is that we may not have a lot of time to do it. The damage we're inflicting may be happening more quickly than we realize—or more slowly. We don't know. Unfortunately, making the transition between discovering problems on this scale and developing the political will and scientific expertise to mitigate them requires a great amount of time—often the better part of a lifetime, at least. Which suggests perhaps the primary charter of universities in the 21st century: to identify the great environmental problems we face, observe them, document them and translate data so that policymakers and the public can institute change.

By virtue of its position on the Pacific Rim as well as its deep reservoir of resources, the University of California is uniquely situated to fulfill this charter. This has long been so, at least since the days in 1944 when Professor John Middleton at UC Riverside discovered that smog was damaging crops in southern California. His discovery led to a research program that eventually became the Statewide Air Pollution Research Center, established in 1961. In fact, the environment has become such an important issue that a new school is being created at UC Santa Barbara, the School of Environmental

Science and Management, to offer graduate-level study. This is the first school of its kind in the UC system, and one of the few in the country, to offer an interdisciplinary approach to applied ecology and management.

In the last 30 years, UC scientists have made a series of remarkable discoveries involving the environment. In 1972, at UC Irvine, Professor Sherwood Rowland and a graduate student named Mario Molina discovered that chlorofluorocarbon atoms released into the atmosphere from such everyday sources as spray cans were rising into the stratosphere, being photolyzed by ultraviolet light, and in the process releasing chlorine atoms.

Those atoms in turn were binding with atoms of ozone. A chain reaction followed, allowing one atom of chlorine to convert literally tens of thousands of protective ozone atoms into ordinary oxygen. Thus the ozone was disappearing. It was of course a landmark moment, one of the most important moments of the 20th century, because for the first time scientists had established a subtle, but clear and present, danger to the global environment. For the first time, the scope of humankind's influence became apparent.

One of the great revelations that scientists have experienced in recent years is that the earth behaves as a coherent "system." As Dr. Kennett puts it, "If you change one part, even slightly, you may see an enormous impact somewhere else. In that sense there's been a broad revolution in the way we think about the earth." Integral to that idea is a new understanding of humankind's place in the system. Just as Newton's law has been gradually modified, Darwin's theory of evolution has begun to be revised as well—not the idea of natural selection, but the idea that humans are the result of a long, steady progression and that humans are somehow special.

Harvard paleontologist Stephen Jay Gould is widely known for his view that evolution takes place as a series of "jumps and starts." The idea is that throughout the planet's history, one catastrophe after another has "reset the clock"—in effect, cut off evolution up to that point, causing the tree of life to begin growing in a slightly different direction. A group of scientists at Berkeley in the late 1970s suggested that such cataclysmic events were caused by the impact of extraterrestrial objects such as meteors or asteroids hitting the earth. In 1989 the Berkeley group acquired new evidence suggesting that at least one such object was a comet. Apparently, the comet smashed into the tip of the Yucatán Peninsula near a place called Chicxulub, blasting a crater 180 kilometers in diameter and creating a tidal wave more than half a mile tall. Much of the water in the Gulf of Mexico was instantaneously displaced and some of it was vaporized, which led to a greenhouse effect that may have lasted for 100,000 years. Earthquakes followed. Some scientists believe it may have taken almost 2 million years for the oceans to reach equilibrium again.

"Darwin taught us that evolution happened slowly and gradually," says Dr. Alejandro Monterar, an Italian geologist who joined the Berkeley group in 1980. "We have gotten used to the belief that the human species is stable, that evolution will go on forever. But in the last 20 years we have begun to see evidence that suggests we are not immune to the pattern of extinction. Impermanence is the real lesson. We know now that mankind may well be temporary—and if we become extinct, it is very natural."

While there is a growing consensus on the need to build our knowledge of the environment, there's disagreement as to what the priorities should be. One problem is that in the case of global warming, for example, human activity may be creating a compensating factor—dust. As we permit overgrazing, erosion, and deforestation, more and more of the land becomes desert; the wind picks up the sand and dust and swirls it into the atmosphere, where it reduces the penetration of sunlight.

"There's a lot of environmental work being done which is big on words and low on facts," says Dr. Walter Monk of the Scripps Institution of Oceanography at UC San Diego. "If I worried about the end of mankind I would worry about forests, food, desertification and overpopulation." Many other environmental scientists agree. Clearly, the growth of population in relation to resources is the most pressing environmental problem of our time.

"I think life on the planet in 70 years is going to be much less comfortable," says Dr. Rowland. "There will be so many more people. Take the island of Haiti, which is already deforested. You have people trying to leave Haiti to find a place where they can survive. I think there will be more and more boat people all over the world. Generally, you have more and more people looking for a higher standard of living. We have a traditional way of getting that standard of living—it's called exploiting natural resources, and dumping the wastes in the atmosphere, in the air and in the ocean. If you continue to have population growth and exploitation, which one will give?"

Such is the doomsday scenario following the end of the Cold War. Not that we'll perish in a nuclear winter, but that our resources will dwindle to nothing. "A change, just by a few degrees," says Dr. Monterar, "could destroy crops and cut the food supply, which could lead to wars and eventually a short-term glaciation that could destroy civilization.

"Sixty million years from now it would appear as a catastrophe, but certainly not nearly as great as the one at the end of the Cretaceous period. There might still be some remnants of our civilization. But much would be lost from the land being eroded and redeposited. If the continents come together, a city on the coast like New York would simply be recycled in the earth's crust. In 40 million years the Himalayas won't be here. No doubt there would be some index fossils of the postmodern era. Roads, artifacts. There would be a chemical record. But it would definitely be a mystery why we disappeared, because on a geological scale these environmental problems we face are unnoticeable. Yes, I think it would be a very long time before they figured out what happened to us."

ABOVE: Cindy Stead surveys the horizon at the Granite Mountains Natural Reserve, an isolated UC research station in southeastern California. Although the reserve is administered by the Riverside campus, biologists and geologists from throughout the UC system come to the station in the East Mojave Desert—occasionally with groups of students—to study the desert ecosystem. "One of the best parts of being here," says Stead's husband and fellow researcher Phillipe Cohen, "is seeing how much the desert affects the attitudes of students who come for the first time. The way they view the world changes profoundly when they realize how much life there is in a place they had imagined was pretty empty."
Photographer: Rick Rickman

TOP: No ordinary rock collection, this sampling gathered by earth sciences graduate student Stuart Gilder came from China to the Paleomagnetism Laboratory at UC Santa Cruz. The lab—one of the few places on earth devoid of magnetic pull—allows researchers to study how the planet's magnetic core has changed over the course of millennia. *Photographer: Jim Gensheimer*

ABOVE: Biologist Dave Herbst takes field notes as part of his research into aquatic insects at the Sierra Nevada Aquatic Research Laboratory, or SNARL, one of the 30 sites in UC's Natural Reserve System. By studying insect life in the waters of Mono County, Herbst says, scientists learn to gauge water quality and understand the impact of drought and geothermal drilling on streams and springs in the eastern Sierra. *Photographer: Rick Rickman*

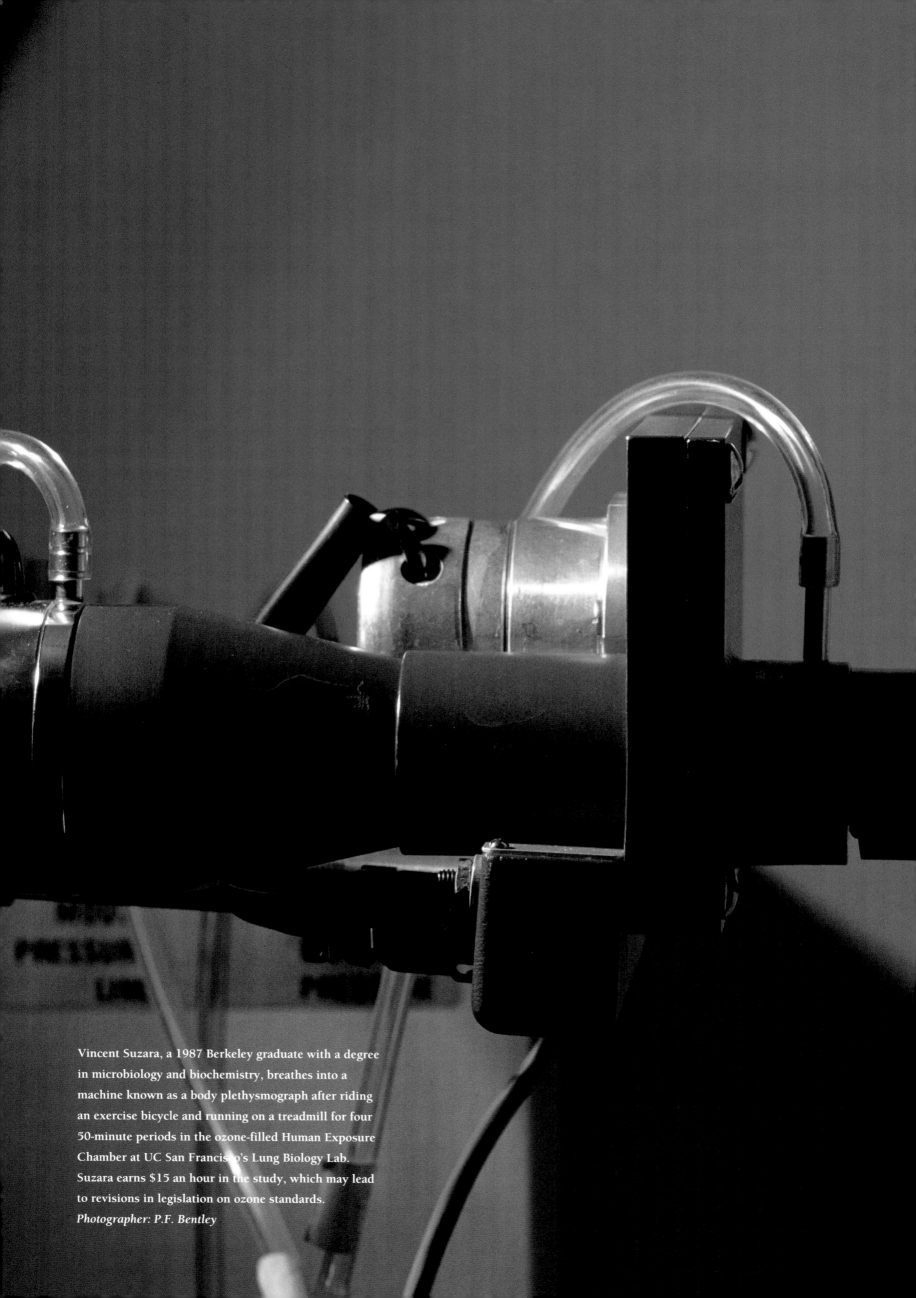

Vincent Suzara, a 1987 Berkeley graduate with a degree
in microbiology and biochemistry, breathes into a
machine known as a body plethysmograph after riding
an exercise bicycle and running on a treadmill for four
50-minute periods in the ozone-filled Human Exposure
Chamber at UC San Francisco's Lung Biology Lab.
Suzara earns $15 an hour in the study, which may lead
to revisions in legislation on ozone standards.
Photographer: P.F. Bentley

ABOVE: Assistant professors Timothy Paine and Jocelyn Millar check on their collection of tree-saving wasps in a special cage at UC Riverside, whose Entomology Department has pioneered research on biological pesticides. The wasps are harmless to humans, but they're a natural enemy of the long-horned borer—a brown and yellow beetle that is killing eucalyptus trees up and down the state. By importing the wasps from Australia and releasing them into the wild, says Millar, "we hope to bring way down the numbers of the long-horned borer."
Photographer: Andy Levin

RIGHT: The Batman of Riverside, assistant professor of biology Roald Roverud, examines a specimen of *Noctiliao albiventris*—otherwise known as the lesser bulldog bat. Roverud has worked with the flying mammals for 12 years, paying particular attention to their use of sonar, or echolocation, as a substitute for sight. By simulating bat echoes, Roverud hopes to learn more precisely how bats process what they hear. The findings are likely to help explain how other animals use their auditory systems, thus aiding scientists to perfect electronic sonar devices.
Photographer: Andy Levin

RIGHT: Twenty feet below the ocean's surface, Mia Tegner explores a kelp forest off Santa Cruz Island, where varied species vie for the light that gives them life. Tegner, a marine biology researcher at the world-renowned Scripps Institution of Oceanography in La Jolla, calls the southern California kelp beds "wonderfully diverse habitats that support hundreds of species of invertebrates, fishes and plants." Weather permitting, Tegner dives once a week; the rest of her time is spent in the laboratory at Scripps, not far from the UC San Diego campus. Tegner's project is one of 250 major research programs currently sponsored by the Scripps Institution, which became part of UC in 1912; others include a plan to monitor the advance of global climate change and a project aimed at mapping the drift of continents.
Photographer: Eric Hanauer

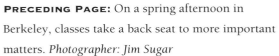

PRECEDING PAGE: On a spring afternoon in Berkeley, classes take a back seat to more important matters. *Photographer: Jim Sugar*

ABOVE AND RIGHT: Splish-splashing and rap dancing in the San Bernardino mountains, kids from urban neighborhoods in southern California enjoy what for many of them is their first time in the great outdoors at the UCLA-run UniCamp. Since 1935, the project has been a labor of love for the UCLA community, which raises most of the yearly $450,000 operating budget with an annual Mardi Gras festival. UCLA students volunteer as counselors for the campers, who are referred by social service agencies in southern California. Once they arrive at UniCamp, the 1,200 campers spend their time swimming, canoeing, hiking, sleeping under the stars and learning arts and crafts. But more important, says counselor Vicki Luce, "they forget whatever problems they face in the outside world for a while so they can just enjoy being kids." *Photographer: Jim Mendenhall*

OVERLEAF: Leslie Graves and Katie Goodchild push for the top as part of the pre-season training regimen for the women's varsity basketball team at Santa Cruz. While sports might be big business at many other campuses, they're strictly for the joy of competition at UCSC; there are no scholarships or grants-in-aid for the school's athletes, who play in the National Collegiate Athletic Association's Division III. And in sharp contrast to team names that evoke images of war and fierceness—Spartans, Trojans or Wildcats, for example—the men and women of Santa Cruz honor one of the less ferocious species found on the campus by calling themselves the Banana Slugs. *Photographer: Jim Gensheimer*

ABOVE RIGHT: Running back Russell White scores a touchdown for the Golden Bears in the Florida Citrus Bowl, a resounding 37-13 win for Cal. The 1991 team was the most successful Bears football team in decades, earning a top-10 national ranking. While men's and women's teams in many sports at Cal have long been among the country's finest, the athletic department's national reputation has suffered because of perennially weak teams in the glamor sports of football and men's basketball. But now, according to Cal Chancellor and sports fan extraordinaire Chang Lin-Tien, "Our aim at Berkeley is to demonstrate that a great academic institution can also have a very strong athletic program." *Photographer: Dan Murphy*

ABOVE: UCLA's Tyus Edney contests a pass by Cal's K.J. Roberts during a Pacific-10 conference game at UCLA's Pauley Pavilion. In 1992, the UCLA team went to the NCAA Tournament for the third year in a row. *Photographer: Jim Mendenhall*

BELOW: Nestled in Strawberry Canyon on the edge of the Cal campus, Memorial Stadium offers Bear backers one of the country's most picturesque locations for a college football field. The stadium, modeled after the Coliseum in Rome, cost nearly a million and a half dollars to construct and was finished just in time for the Big Game with Stanford in 1923—which Cal won 9-0. Since then, crowds in excess of 80,000 have jammed their way into Memorial Stadium nearly 20 times, despite the fact that its official capacity is listed as 75,662. *Photographer: Barrie Rokeach*

ABOVE AND TOP RIGHT: All the world's a stage—
even the redwood groves at UC Santa Cruz, where student Darius Stone takes to the air in rehearsals for his
role as Mustard Seed in Shakespeare's *A Midsummer
Night's Dream*. With the help of a mountain-climbing
harness connected to a rope-and-pulley system, constructed during a six-week period amidst the trees that
dominate the central part of the campus, Stone and his
fellow fairies presented audiences with quite a sight:

"When you see four men in tutus flying around,"
says Stone, "it's kinda funny." Each summer since
1981, UCSC has sponsored a theater festival known
as Shakespeare Santa Cruz, featuring modern inter-
pretations of plays by the bard as well as works by
other noted playwrights. Professional actors share
the spotlight with students, providing inspiration:
"I'd like to be able to do this for a living," says Stone,
"and be a big star." *Photographer: Jim Gensheimer*

ABOVE: Riverside students pause between classes to sign a petition for a state ballot initiative designed to mandate environmentally sound logging practices. The Riverside campus has the smallest student body of the eight general-education schools in the system, with an undergraduate enrollment of fewer than 9,000 students; UC officials, however, expect that number to double by the year 2005.
Photographer: Andy Levin

OVERLEAF: Volunteers for the United Farm Workers union staff a table at Riverside's Commons Cafeteria. The UFW's goal, as spelled out on the banner behind Jorge Sanchez and Stephanie Orr, is "a safe and just food supply," including better working conditions for the grape pickers and other field workers who form a vital human component of California's agricultural economy. *Photographer: Andy Levin*

"Our
and
No was!

Boycott! GRAPES
No Grapes

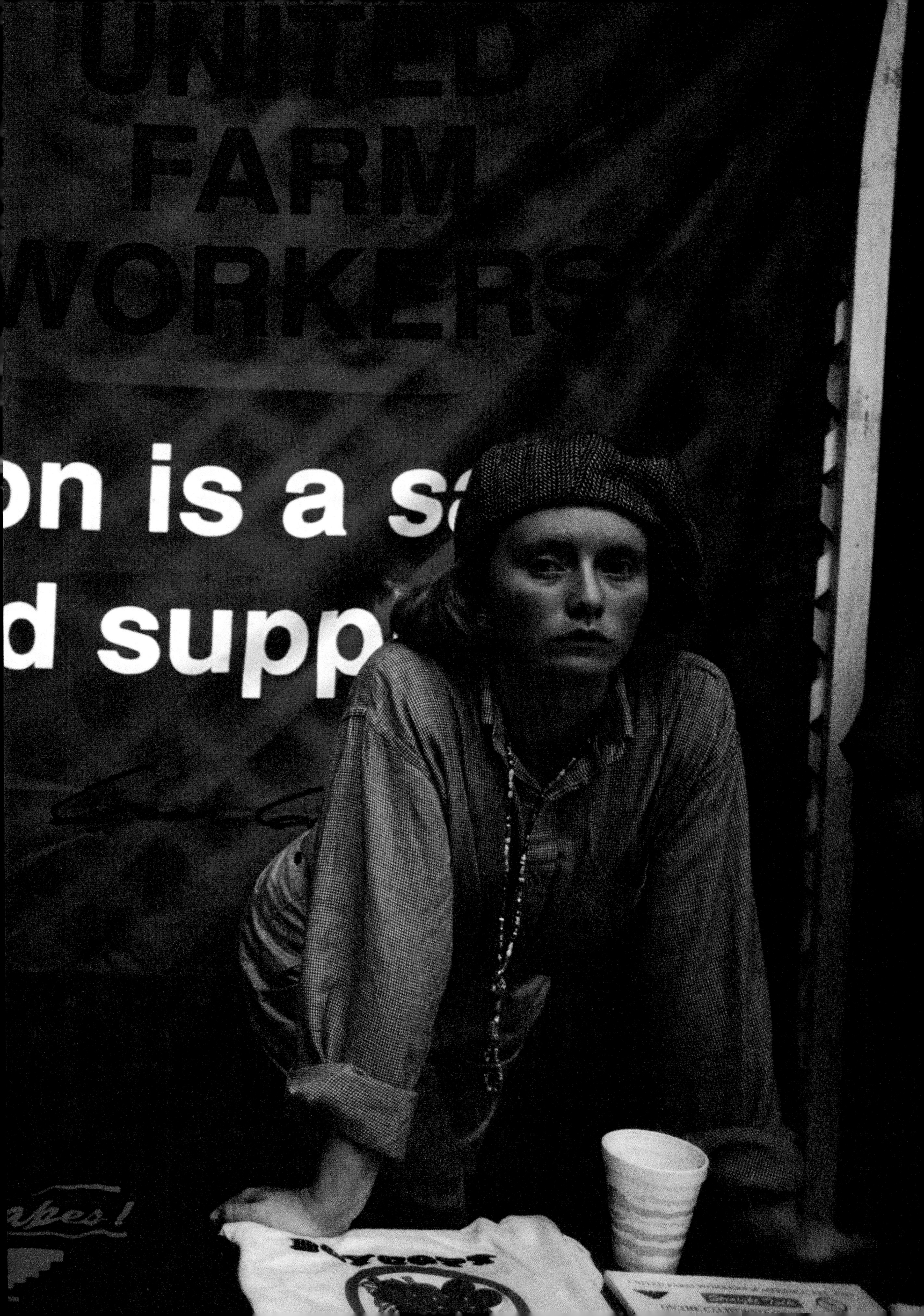
UNITED
FARM
WORKERS
on is a sa
d supp

Berkeley

Davis

Irvine

Los Angeles

Riverside

San Diego

San Francisco

Santa Barbara

Santa Cruz

THE APPLE, THE WORM, AND ORIGINAL SIN

The story of the fruit which the serpent gave to Eve, and she to Adam, was first written down in approximately 1000 B.C. It was based on an oral tradition that may have begun in Sumer. There was no mention of an apple in the original story, and no suggestion of sin. In fact, it wasn't until 1,400 years later, in A.D. 400, when Christians translated the story into Latin, that the correlation of the apple with sex and sin was made. As it turns out, the word for evil in Latin is *malum*; the word for apple, *malus*. Many scholars believe the apple has become the symbol for original sin and bliss gone bad through a linguistic coincidence.

The irony is that the original fruit in the myth could well have been an apple, which has been the most widely eaten fruit in the world for millennia. Indeed, the apples growing in the Fertile Crescent in 1000 B.C. were descendants of still more ancient apples from the southern Caucasus, probably from the southern part of the former Soviet republic called Kazakhstan, a mountainous place first inhabited by nomads from Mongolia. It's possible that the apple originates in an area of Kazakhstan called Alma Ata, which by various translations means "mother apple" or "father apple."

From there, still in prehistoric times, apples spread west, with one notable exception—a region of China called Xinjiang, north of Tibet. They thrived in southern Europe and around the Mediterranean. The apple eventually spread north, where it flourished in Germany and Great Britain. Then, along with the colonists, and a governor named Endicott, it arrived in Massachusetts in the early 1600s. Some 200 years after that, in the 1850s, the apple could be found on the West Coast, mostly in Washington and Oregon and along the coast of California in Sebastopol and Watsonville.

These days, 50 percent of American apples are grown in the West, where they represent a $1.1 billion industry. In California, apples are a relatively minor crop, after grapes, almonds, and walnuts. The average income of an apple grower—large companies aside—is around $30,000 a year. In the great scheme of things in California, apples are peanuts. But sustaining the apple industry demands solutions to problems that characterize California agriculture in general and research at the University of California in particular.

Over the years, UC scientists have been involved with a kaleidoscope of new developments—crops that thrive with little water; a bacterium used to inhibit frost in various vegetables; a computer program to help growers manage cotton production. But of all the agricultural research going on at UC, perhaps the most interesting is the Integrated Pest Management program, which is the largest and most advanced program of its kind in the world and includes more than 150 UC scientists in more than a dozen departments on three campuses.

With the urbanization of California have come hundreds of species of plants and animals, many of which pose enduring threats to agriculture. Exotic pests account for 67 percent of reported crop losses. But at the same time, the era of pesticides is passing. Consumer concern with food safety, worker health and the environment—a movement which began largely in cities—has spread to farms, leading to the enlistment of a variety of Orwellian-sounding solutions including natural predators, parasites, microorganisms and genetically engineered plants. In the last decade, among many advances, UC scientists have pioneered the use of alfalfa strips in cotton fields as a way of housing the western predatory mite, which feeds on various spidermite species that eat the cotton. Genetic engineers have designed a mothproofing gene for walnuts; scientists at UC Davis came up with a natural predator for the tomato fruit worm; and entomologists at Riverside have imported parasitic wasps from Israel to slay the pernicious ash whitefly.

Which brings us back to the apple, and the worm.

LEFT: A university invention bears fruit as it harvests in the fields of Yolo County. The automated tomato harvester, the 1959 brainchild of UC Davis agricultural engineering professor Coby Lorenzen, picks and sorts an average of 35 tons of tomatoes an hour.
Photographer: Jack Clark/Comstock

In the original myth of Adam and Eve, the serpent was a mysterious symbol of sexual power and spirituality. In Genesis, the serpent was cast as a smooth-talking beelzebub. But in both stories the serpent lived in the garden, not in the fruit, despite some artists' depictions of a boa-sized worm.

The worm longest known to inhabit the apple is the larva of the codling moth, which as an adult is a dark gray and brown little beast with coppery markings and a 2/3-inch wingspan. While California apples are besieged by 32 insect pests and eight diseases, there is no threat so familiar, or battle so thankless, as that presented by this homely moth. A "meddler" was how the Roman writer Cliny described it.

Aside from apples, in California the meddler attacks pears, prunes, plums and walnuts. First the female codling moth lays between 30 and 70 eggs on the foliage. The eggs transform into larvae that make their way to the apples, then bore to the core. Once grown, the larvae leave the fruit, wiggle down the tree trunk and burrow beneath the bark where they spin cocoons. One day they transform into pupae and flutter away. All in four weeks, the greatest damage occurring between April and July.

Chuck O'Rear

Why does the worm have such a need for the apple? The answer is that the larvae are drawn to a chemical called beta-farnesene, which the apple releases as it matures. In effect, you could say that the codling moth has a chemical dependency problem with apple juice.

The codling moth is one of the few pests that has been able to survive all-out chemical war, including nicotine and lead arsenic in the '40s and '50s, and DDT in the '60s. Lately it seems the moth has even developed a tolerance for Guthion, the trade name for several organic compounds that for the last 20 years have been generally effective in killing it. Even with insecticides, some farmers report 10 and 20 percent crop losses in the last year; they usually expect no more than 15 percent and push for less than five percent. As a result of the resurgence, there are half a dozen scientists at four UC campuses experimenting with different methods of control. One key lies in Kazakhstan, where there's very little damage done to apples by the codling moth. The same is true in the Chinese region of Xinjiang. That's because of the presence of a very specialized parasitic wasp, which some scientists think will be a promising natural deterrent to the codling moth in America.

Andy Levin

"I'm just in the process of bringing the first batch of these natural enemies into the country to see what effect they might have," says Nick Mills, a Berkeley entomologist. "But it will be another year or two before we know anything. Our hope is to develop a reasonably priced, long-term alternative control." This first batch of wasps includes one species from the Crimea, another from France.

Besides wasps, scientists are working with sex pheromones, a novel approach with broad potential for a variety of pests. When the female codling moth emerges from the bark she emits a scent that attracts the male. Scientists have discovered how to create a synthetic scent that can be sprayed on the trees so that the male can't find the female. This synthetic scent is in the process of being registered with the FDA, though major problems with release systems and dissipation still exist. And then there are viruses, fungi and bacteria, which are now increasingly popular. These are perhaps the most controversial controls and, like nuclear power, they offer prospects of both panacea and plague. In the case of apples, use of the granulosis virus was first proposed in 1969 by professor Lou Falcon at UC Berkeley, but promising results in laboratory orchards have not been duplicated in commercial applications, and the potential remains unclear.

Of 400 insects targeted in the last 100 years, only about 15 to 20 percent have been successfully controlled by any method. Scientists still don't know why pests respond to some controls and not others. "You're not going to find just one thing to solve the pest problem," says Lyn Garling, an entomologist at UC Santa Cruz. She is working on still another codling-moth control involving nematodes, microscopic round worms that eat the larvae. "It will take a whole regime of different organisms. There is no silver bullet."

Chuck O'Rear

I f the theological problem is that Adam and Eve ate the apple, the agricultural problem is that we took the apples out of the garden, away from Alma Ata, and tried to grow them outside their natural environment. This notion of agricultural "original sin" leads to the very modern revelation on the part of an increasing number of researchers, farmers and policymakers that the future of agriculture lies in restoring the natural environment as much as possible. That in turn means redefining what we as a society need to sustain ourselves and what processes will help us do that most efficiently.

This whole idea is encoded in a relatively new term, "sustainable agriculture," which was coined at UC Davis and means different things to different people but suggests generally the goal of living within our ecological means. The consensus among many at UC is that right now we in California are pressing our luck. Soil fertility is declining in some areas. Water salinity is increasing; the damage to ground water around Fresno is well known, and, according to one 1987 report, more than 3,000 water wells have been shut down in California primarily because of salinity problems.

Jim Gensheimer

"I don't think there's a viable alternative to sustainable agriculture," says Benny Fouche, a staff research associate in the entomology department of the UC Cooperative Extension at Berkeley. He's also a former pear grower. "But it's going to mean revising the view that we've got to get every last ounce of productivity out of the land—maximum production, maximum yields, maximum pesticides—the hell with the next generation. Too many farmers are taking the land for granted on the assumption that if they can just hold on to it long enough, they can sell it to developers."

But how can the attitudes of farmers be changed?

Carolyn Pickel is an entomologist long familiar with apples and codling moths, and a farm advisor with the UC Cooperative Extension: "Farmers have different personalities. For example, walnut growers understand biological

controls because it has worked for them. Apple growers have seen less success and so they're more wary. I think growers will become more open to change as they see results, and as they understand that they may not have to spray as much as they thought—that taking a sample [of pests] in an orchard is the first step toward sustainable agriculture. In fact, spraying without determining exactly what the threat is has been a major cause in increasing pest resistance."

Reversing current trends probably means that the farmer will have to pay more to produce his product, and the consumer more to eat it. The immediate question may be, how much are we willing to pay for food that comes from a holistic

Dana Fineman

approach to farming? But in the longer term, the question reverses: how long can we really afford the chemical and hydrological largesse we now take for granted?

"Our charge is to feed people, and we're looking at incredible increases in population—seven billion by 2000," says Hal Carter, professor of agricultural economics and director of the Agricultural Issues Center at UC Davis. "That would seem to imply we must produce a lot more food. At the same time, environmental issues are near the top of our list of priorities as a society. How do we do both? Part of the answer—and the challenge—lies in adapting technology to a sustainable agricultural system on the one hand, and still providing an adequate amount of food on the other."

As for the apple, its future may be bleak in California. Ironically, apple growers were among the first to endorse organic farming in California in the 1970s. But now apple juice from Argentina has undercut the apple industry in Watsonville. Urban sprawl and increasing land values are devouring apple orchards in Sebastapol. Apples grown in the Central Valley are losing their competitive edge to apples from Washington, where land, water and labor are all cheaper.

Of course all of that was as nothing in Eden and will be so again. Wasps or no wasps, Guthion or no Guthion, sooner or later the apple will find its proper place in the world once more, decades of human intervention notwithstanding. California farmers will rediscover the joys of growing their crops in acceptance of the facts of land and water that surround us. Our apples may come to us once more from Alma Ata. And no sooner will that happy day arrive, perhaps, than the codling moth will join the list of endangered species.

BELOW: Helping the state's farmers keep their fruit fresh and colorful, Carlos Crisosto holds two handfuls of peaches while huddling with growers at the Kaprielian Brothers automated fruit-packing plant in Parlier. Crisosto is a post- harvest specialist with UC's Cooperative Extension office in Kearney, one of 63 offices around the state that counsels farmers on a wide variety of agricultural issues.
Photographer: Chuck O'Rear

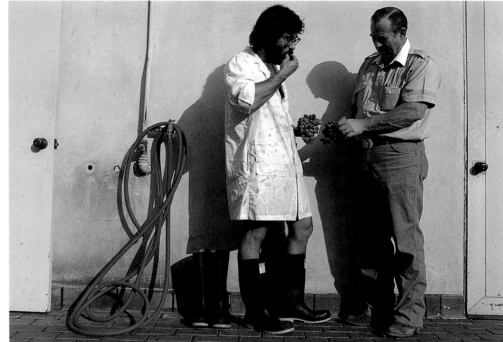

TOP: Passing this chemistry class at Santa Cruz may be simply a matter of taste, as Stacey Chako and David Jon Mould find out during a lecture session. While students at UC Davis can choose from more than two dozen wine-related classes, UCSC students are limited to a single course, An Analytical View of Wines and Wine Chemistry. The class, one of many that fulfills a UCSC science requirement, teaches students how to make wine and identify its key organic compounds. But the real goal, according to chemistry professor Phil Crews, is to "attract nonscience majors into a class where they can learn what the scientific method is all about." *Photographer: Jim Gensheimer*

ABOVE: Staff research associate Walter Winton pauses for a grape-tasting moment with Davis graduate student Scott Rich during the October crush at UC Davis, when graduate and undergraduate students pitch in to help the Department of Viticulture and Enology harvest grapes from 80 acres of UC-owned vineyards. The California wine industry depends on scientists at Davis to develop techniques in viticulture and enology, but it needn't worry about competition from campus winemakers: By state law, wine produced at the university must be either used for research purposes or destroyed. *Photographer: Annie Griffiths Belt*

ABOVE AND RIGHT: Former farmworker Jenny Rodriguez, a program representative for the Agricultural Health and Safety Center at UC Davis, interviews field workers in a pistachio orchard in Madera County. Determined to reduce injuries and illness among farmworkers, Rodriguez finds out what workers know—and, more important, don't know—about working with and around pesticides. She then helps prepare safety-training seminars, videos and brochures. Her task is not an easy one: "How do you instill the need to slow down," she asks, "when people are being paid by the piece?" Nonetheless, she says each day is full of rewards. "Having come myself from an extremely harsh migrant seasonal farmworker background, I find it incredibly satisfying to have the opportunity to in some small way be a positive influence. There are times when I ask myself, 'Am I getting paid for this? I should be paying the university.'" *Photographer: Jim Gensheimer*

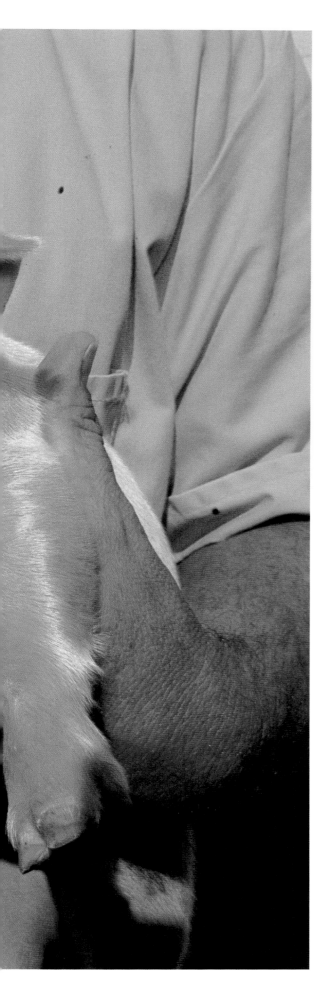

ABOVE: A hardy soul puts a well-protected hand into one of a cow's three stomachs at Picnic Day, UC Davis' annual open house. Eight cows at Davis have holes with removeable stoppers in their sides, making it possible for researchers to look directly into the animals' digestive systems. According to Brandt Keuscher, a dairy herdsman at the university, the hole causes the cow no discomfort. Most of the bacteria in the cow's 50-gallon first stomach, he says, is resistant to being killed by exposure to the air—or the plastic-covered hand of an inquisitive undergrad. *Photographer: P.F. Bentley*

LEFT: Stanford University in Palo Alto may be known as the Farm, but the nickname is far better suited to UC Davis, where students can study, among many other subjects, animal nutrition, animal physiology, animal biochemistry, animal genetics and all aspects of farm management. About a thousand piglets are born each year at the hog barn on campus. "California may be a minor hog state," says Hubert Heitman, professor emeritus of animal science, "but we still need a hog barn. Our ag students can't afford to be without experience in handling swine." *Photographer: P.F. Bentley*

LEFT: Tomato librarian Charles Rick flips through the seed packets in a vault at UC Davis. The self-described "tomato aficionado," a Davis professor for more than 50 years, spent much of his academic career traveling the globe in search of new tomato strains. He now works with several research associates to maintain the collection of seeds, representing more than 2,000 varieties of tomato—the most diverse tomato-seed library on the planet. Requests for seeds pour into Rick's Tomato Genetics Resource Center from scientists around the world; most come from people aiming to engineer new varieties of tomato, replant varieties that no longer grow in the wild or study how to make tomatoes more pest- and drought-resistant. *Photographer: Chuck O'Rear*

BELOW LEFT: Lucia Borello and Faud Bin Aziz clear the weeds at the Student Farm at UC Santa Cruz. Borello and Bin Aziz are among the 30 students enrolled each year in the Ecological Horticulture Apprenticeship Program, in which participants study organic farming inside the classroom and out in UCSC's 25-acre farm and four-acre garden. The apprenticeship program is one of several parts of UCSC's innovative Agroecology Program, which aims to encourage "sustainable" agriculture—a way of protecting natural resources while keeping production levels high. Many of the students come from developing countries, to which they hope to return and apply the principles of agroecology on a wide scale. *Photographer: Jim Gensheimer*

RIGHT: Shopping for organic produce grown on campus, Santa Cruz student Eric Pape reaps the benefits of the UCSC farm and garden. Apprentices in the Ecological Horticulture Program sell their fruits and vegetables at a farmers' market twice a week, raising money to keep their program afloat while obtaining hands-on marketing experience. *Photographer: Jim Gensheimer*

LEFT: The living is easy at Santa Barbara's Alumni Vacation Center, where UC alumni from throughout the system gather every summer to spend a week swimming, playing tennis or golf, reading, listening to special faculty lectures or doing absolutely nothing, all with the added incentive of all-day child care. Much like the Lair of the Bear camp run by the Berkeley Alumni Association in the Sierra foothills, the Santa Barbara vacation center is just the place for parents and kids to go off to summer camp—together. *Photographer: Jim Mendenhall*

ABOVE: Students begging a teacher for a better grade? No, they're simply studying the Iyengar method of Hatha Yoga at the East Fieldhouse in Santa Cruz. The university offers no credit for the classes in yoga—a Sanskrit word meaning "uniting the self with the universe"—but the rewards are ample: "I notice a kind of mental clarity when I do yoga," says one student. "It really helps bring me into balance." *Photographer: Jim Gensheimer*

OVERLEAF: Esther Williams lives! Four members of Berkeley's synchronized-swimming team practice at the Hearst Gym's North Pool, where they spend several hours a day during the three-month competitive season. Besides creativity, says club president Jennifer Troth, the sport requires "strength, flexibility and cardiovascular endurance." *Photographer: Marcia Lippman*

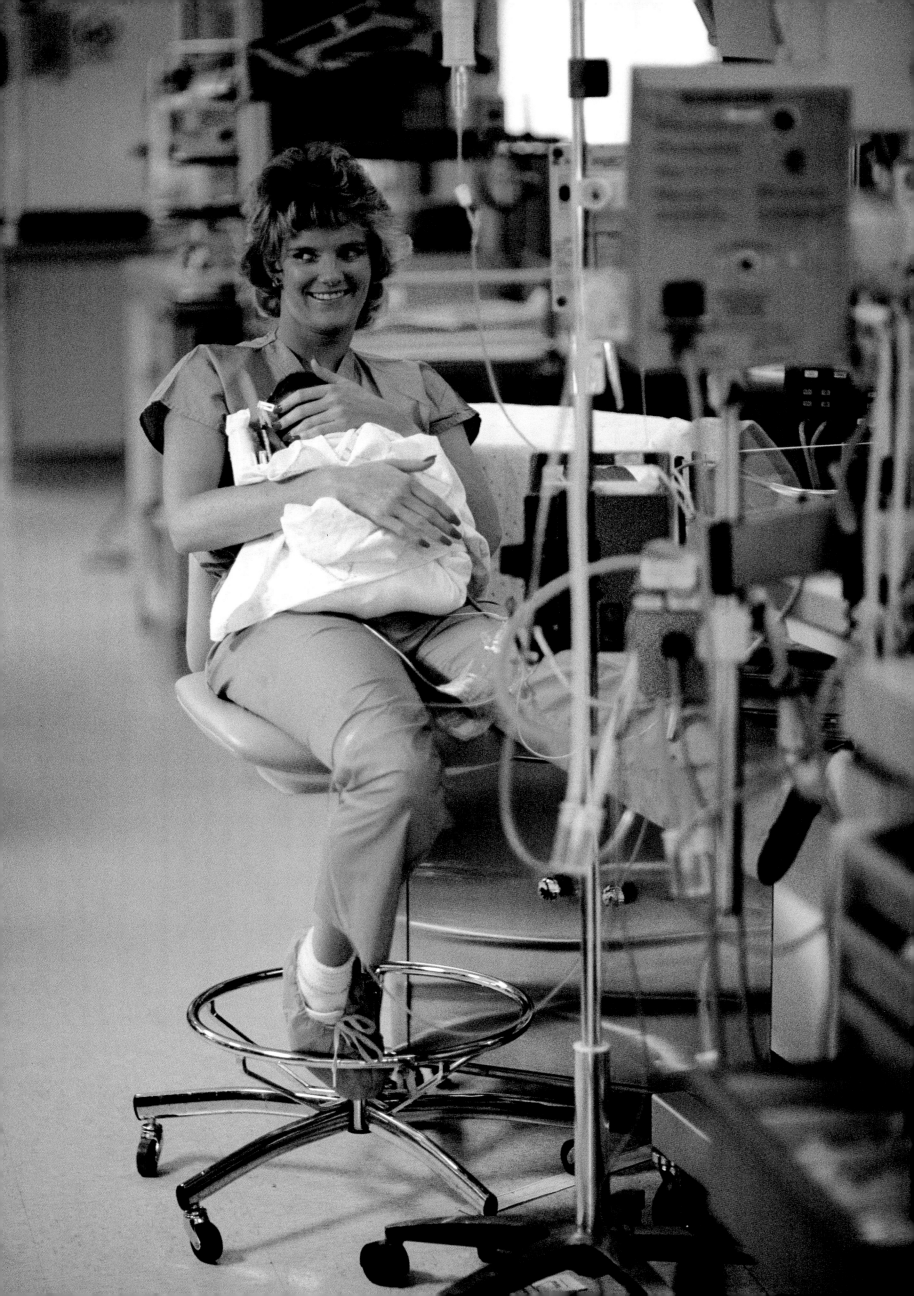

THE FAITH OF THE HEALER

I f one's life were to be measured as the sum of extraordinary moments, then doctors—along with soldiers—must have the greatest sum. Both live among moments thick with the unusual, and always with the possibility of revelation. According to an acquaintance who is a surgeon and a former Green Beret, "In both 'theaters,' you're on that edge where death is watching you and you're watching death. In a sense, you're having a conversation, you're becoming familiar with each other. It's in those moments when I feel the greatest intimacy with life. But there is a difference. When you're a soldier the moment is excruciating and heady—sometimes, in retrospect, even intoxicating. But as a doctor, I've found that during that moment when I'm with death, with someone who's dying, it makes me feel very, very humble."

Doctors work at the intersection of the great thematic lines of the age—Technology, Health, and the Individual—all braced with an underlying sense of optimism that science will ultimately find a solution to keep life going. Perhaps that's why the new immune-related diseases such as AIDS, and those looming environmental questions about resource and ozone depletion, seem so sinister—the solutions seem beyond our capability. It's as though Nature were shaking her weary head and saying to humankind, "You think you know it all, but even with all your cleverness you cannot be free of me. You cannot escape all the parts of yourself so easily."

Yet you go into a medical school at a place like the University of California—at any one of five campuses—and there is the constant illusion that doctors do know it all. This illusion of power is reinforced by the ubiquity of technology, and news of the newest miracle cure, as well as by the sheer number of cases in which lives have been prolonged or saved.

Consider a few of the most recent breakthroughs. At UCLA's Clinical Research Center, doctors are experimenting with an antibody developed in mice to fight oncogenes. The antibody fastens onto a tumor cell in such a way as to block it from receiving the substances it needs to grow. This antibody may be effective in treating several kinds of cancer.

At UC Irvine—which incidentally is where the first implantable insulin pump was given to a patient—psychiatry professor Monte S. Buchsbaum and a team of doctors and scientists are finding answers to such questions as whether autism is a form of schizophrenia or an unrelated disorder; and whether there is a difference between the brain waves of normal people and those of people with schizophrenia or Parkinson's disease.

In the department of orthopedics at UC San Diego, doctors are developing equipment and procedures to measure an individual's strength at various points in a range of motion following back injury, forming the basis of a "resistance exercise" schedule. "The significance," says Dr. Vert Mooney, "is not only in terms of costs savings—back pain accounts for 40 percent of worker's compensation costs—but also in duration of treatment."

And at UC Davis, Dr. Hap Paul has pioneered use of an IBM robot to drill the sockets for artificial-hip implants. Whereas previously the surgeon's equivalent of a hammer and chisel had been used, resulting in a poor fit between the metal implant and the living bone, Paul's precision technique improves the stability of the implant, reduces pain after surgery and enhances the patient's ability to walk.

Less traditional forms of medical research take place at UC as well. At UC Berkeley, there is a project to identify plant species used by the Maya Indians for medicinal purposes. It is a collaboration with Mexico's Chiapas State Department of Public Health, and preliminary findings are promising.

Beyond these examples, which are merely representative of many other high-profile breakthroughs, there are a hundred more subtle examples—advances and refinements in surgery techniques, training, equipment and organizational structure—all of which contribute to this tremendous confidence and optimism bestowed on doctors.

LEFT: Premature babies are in good hands in Irvine Medical Center's neonatal intensive care unit, headed by pediatrics professor Louis Gluck. Gluck established the world's first neonatal intensive care unit in 1960, earning him widespread recognition as the father of neonatalogy. *Photographer: Paul Kennedy*

But underlying all the breakthroughs is the relationship between doctor and patient, those extraordinary moments that transcend technology and emanate from sympathy, insight and the need for care. Dr. Sharon Brooks-Fujikawa, an audiologist at UCI, remembers the moment when a 26-year-old Vietnamese patient called her on the telephone. It was the first time the man had been able to use a remarkable new device, a 22-electrode transducer placed in the inner ear and connected to a computer. The computer translates sound into electrical impulses, which the electrodes pick up as frequencies. The inner ear can then "hear" and recognize those frequencies. "The point that summarizes where this patient is now," says Brooks-Fujikawa, "is that he's teaching guitar."

Dr. Jack Lake, who specializes in liver transplants at UC San Francisco—one of the top five liver transplant centers in the country—remembers the 19-year-old girl who came into the hospital with fulminant liver failure. She died 36 hours later because no organ donor could be found and because her own liver deteriorated so quickly. "It was especially tragic," says Dr. Lake, "because we've been able to get liver transplants for 70 percent of those who need them, and of those there is a 90 percent survival rate. This was heartbreaking. I have three daughters myself. But the one positive aspect is that the knowledge we gained from her death will help save her sister, who suffers from the same problem."

Dr. Michael Harrison, professor of pediatric surgery at UC San Francisco, thinks of a whole series of moments with one patient, a pregnant mother in North Carolina. She's carrying a fetus with a diaphragmatic hernia, a condition that affects one fetus in 2,000. While the problem can be dealt with after birth, it is better and cheaper to deal with it before the child is born. Unfortunately, that requires money the family doesn't have. Their one hope is to take advantage of a National Institutes of Health grant to UCSF to study this very procedure. But while the grant has been made on paper, NIH doesn't

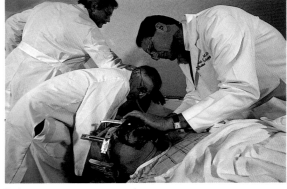

Jim Sugar

have the funding to follow through. Meanwhile, the small town where the family lives is trying to raise money through car washes and bake sales. "They're determined to come out here," says Dr. Harrison, "but the timing may not be quite right."

And then there is a moment from Dr. Bruce Achauer's collection. Dr. Achauer is an associate professor of plastic surgery at UC Irvine and director of the UCI Burn Center. It was in March, 1977, a Sunday evening after a rainy day. Dr. Achauer was at a meeting of the Hand Society, a group of plastic surgeons in Irvine, and was speaking with a colleague when he got a call that a very badly burned six-year-old boy had just arrived in the emergency room.

The little boy, David Rothenberg, had planned to go to Disneyland with his father that day. But then it rained, they couldn't go, and for some reason not being able to go enraged the boy's father. At the end of the day he poured gasoline over his son and lit a match to it. Eventually neighbors arrived, then an ambulance. At the hospital, it was determined that the boy had burns over 90 percent of his body—mostly third-degree burns.

"At that point we didn't know this was part of an assault," remembers Dr. Achauer. "It was simply a burn case, but one in which there didn't seem to be much hope. I remember someone saying, 'Well, there's no chance of his surviving.' But I was a young, very gung-ho surgeon and I was thinking, 'But of course he's got a chance to survive.' And we set to work. He had severe inhalation injuries, but we got through that. We took away some burned skin and grafted new skin from a cadaver. And then at one point the kidneys stopped. But we got those going again. We fought a whole series of battles and a couple of times he was close to death and it could have gone either way—it's an enormously complicated struggle you're waging, dealing with immunity problems, the pulmonary system, and then the surgery, all the timing and coordinating, but we did it."

For the 15 years since then, Dr. Achauer and a team of physicians have been helping to restore David Rothenberg's body. "David has shown great maturity and equally great compassion," says Dr. Achauer. "What's been spectacular is getting to know David, watching him grow up. We go to basketball games together. He's been extraordinary. We're about to rebuild his nose and scalp."

Dr. Achauer adds that one of the most important lessons of this experience for him has been a new understanding of pain: "It's not true that one becomes better able to tolerate pain. I think what we're learning is to be more liberal with medication. We

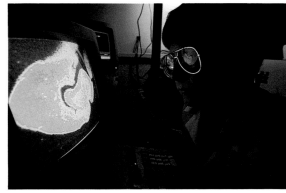

need to be more sympathetic to pain. As doctors, we often think we can tell when someone's in real pain, but what we're learning is to keep asking, and then give as much medication as a patient wants." Addiction in this kind of case is not an issue.

I

t's an odd idea to think that doctors still have anything to learn about pain or that they might not be sympathetic to it. Until about 1910, comforting the patient was often all a doctor could do. From surgery to psychology, the available knowledge was severely limited, and usually cut with uncertainty over religious and social issues. But since then, the doctor has been gradually separated from his patient—by technology, bureaucracy, lifestyle and an education that stresses knowledge more than personal care.

Lately, humanism has crept back into the curricula. Today, for example, out of approximately 125 medical schools in this country, more than 80 have staff who teach the metaphysical aspects of medicine. One of the people who began this movement was David Duncombe. While teaching anatomy at Yale in the mid-'60s, he started the Society for Health and Human Values, initially "a sort of old-boy's club of theologians and medical school deans who were interested in bringing ethics and religion to medicine. It's still a kind of underground, existentialist movement among physicians and medical

students," says Duncombe, who until recently taught anatomy at UCSF. He is now director of the Landberg Center for Health and Ministry, a private organization serving UCSF. "The idea is to get students to think about human life and to keep in mind the spiritual values of medicine."

Understanding the patient's role as a partner in healing may actually be one of the most important breakthroughs going on in medicine these days. It's also a new role for the doctor—to educate the patient not only to his or her role in planning a course of action, but also in developing a positive attitude. Dr. Charles Wilson is a neurosurgeon at UCSF, an ultramarathoner, and a legend nationally and internationally. Among his achievements as a doctor, he developed an innovative technique called the trans-sphanoidal approach, in which a surgeon reaches a brain tumor by going through the nose and sinuses rather than the skull.

In recent years Dr. Wilson has begun to revise his view of patient attitude as a factor in healing. Principally, two events caused the change. The first involved a colleague, a heart surgeon, who had a recurrence of a 10-year-old case of malignant melanoma. He entered the hospital and within a couple of weeks was dead—after it appeared he had weathered his illness. "I have dark skin and a number of moles," explains Dr. Wilson. "The following Monday [after the colleague's death] I met a dermatologist and had him look at some suspicious areas. I also told him about our mutual colleague and he explained that this man, in the weeks before the recurrence of his melanoma, had had a series of professional crises. The dermatologist had seen this phenomenon before: low body resistance, a series of personal crises, followed by a recurrence."

The other event occurred after he gave a speech at a national conference on brain tumors. Several of his patients attended. "After my address, I went down to shake hands and hug my patients, and it suddenly occurred to me that the reason they were still alive was because they all had this very strong belief that they were going to get well. They could look at themselves in the mirror and say, 'The odds aren't good, but I'm going to beat it.'"

Dr. Wilson says these experiences have given him insight into how to approach not only his own life, but also the lives of his patients: "I've always told my patients, 'One, I'm a perpetual optimist.

Two, you've got a serious disease but you're going to get the very best treatment available, and I don't know if I can cure you, but that's my intention.' These are people without a snowball's chance of making it.

"Now I tell them all that but I also say, 'It's very important for you to truly *believe*, not just say, but truly believe that you're going to be cured—because I can tell you from personal experience that if you don't think you'll be cured, you don't have a chance.' It's not psychotherapy. I'm not trying to get them pumped up. It's not whistling in the dark. And I don't look out the window when I say this. I pull up close and look them in the eye. And I'm very convincing because I truly believe it. It's really up to the patient to develop that inner strength, which is the real source of healing."

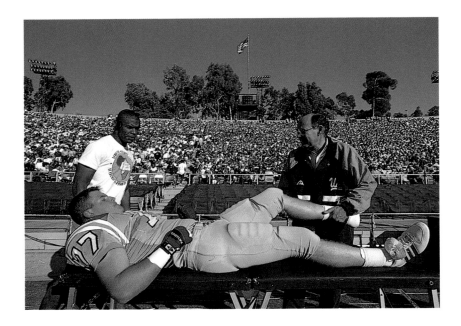

Top: Doctor to the weekend warriors, Gerald
Finerman tests the knee of UCLA's Eric Banducci as
teammate Marvin Goodwin looks on during a Bruin
home game at the Rose Bowl in Pasadena. Finerman,
professor of orthopedic surgery and director of the
sports-medicine program at UCLA Medical Center,
says UCLA is a national leader in the study of sports
medicine in large part because "we're one of the few
schools with both a medical center on campus and a
highly competitive department of intercollegiate
athletics." *Photographer: Mark Wexler*

Above: A hearing test is fun for young Joshua
Beltram as he sits on his mother's lap at UC San
Diego's Audiology Clinic—where the sound monitor
and colorful pegboard help Joshua signal to audiologist Genevieve Newman that he's heard a sound.
Patients from throughout San Diego County use the
clinic at the UCSD School of Medicine, renowned
for its pioneering use of cochlear implants that allow
the deaf to hear. In an example of intercampus coop-
eration, the multichannel cochlear implant was
developed at UC San Francisco and subsequently
introduced at UCSD. *Photographer: Dana Fineman*

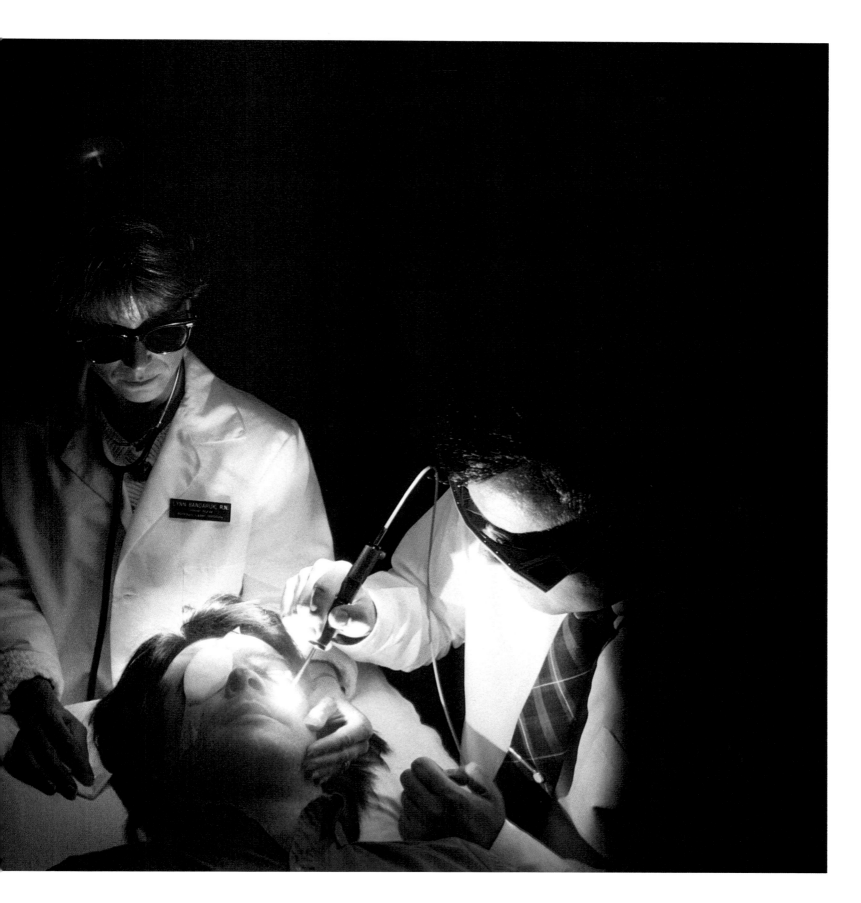

ABOVE: It may look like a magic wand, but the tool in Dr. Jay Nelson's hand is simply a product of modern medical technology: a laser, which is being used to remove a patient's birthmark in a painless 15-minute operation. Nelson and his colleagues at UC Irvine's Beckman Laser Institute and Medical Clinic use lasers to unclog arteries, break up kidney stones, clear cataracts and study the inner workings of cells. The world's first research center dedicated exclusively to the study of lasers in biomedicine, Beckman adds a futuristic touch to the College of Medicine at Irvine, one of the five medical schools in the UC system. *Photographer: Rick Rickman*

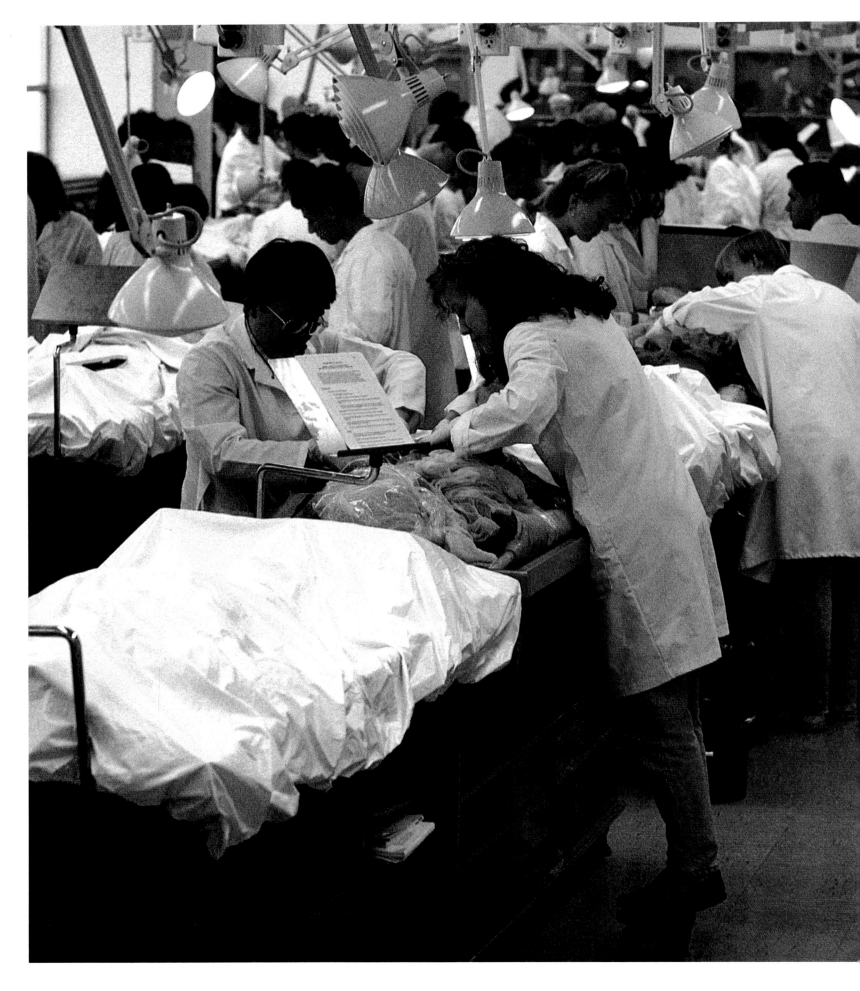

ABOVE: Medicine is no profession for the squeamish, as these students at UC San Francisco find out in their Anatomy 100A class. Much of the class time is spent dissecting cadavers willed to the university; before the students make their first cut, however, they hear from second-year students, who warn them that the experience might be unsettling. "When people see cadavers for the first time," says adjunct professor Sexton Sutherland, "they naturally reflect on their own mortality. So we try to teach them how to deal with their emotions." The Anatomy 100A course at UCSF—a campus composed entirely of schools of medicine, dentistry, nursing and pharmacy—is entitled Gross Anatomy because the students take the long view, studying bodies with the naked eye rather than with a microscope. *Photographer: P.F. Bentley*

ABOVE: Four-time UC Irvine Teacher of the Year James Fallon hands out knowledge and enthusiasm for learning to students in his Gross Anatomy class. Fallon's area of expertise is the brain; he relishes his work with students in Gross Anatomy, he says, because "teaching all the parts and systems of the body keeps me refreshed." Fallon adds that he tries to make learning fun, especially for first-year medical students, who are "extremely stressed because they're so swamped with information."
Photographer: Paul Kennedy

OVERLEAF: It's not such a long leap from jumping jacks in the mountains to improvements in the operating room—at least not for UC San Francisco's Dr. John Severinghaus, who monitors the heartbeat and oxygen intake of post-doctoral fellow Marlowe Eldridge in an early-morning exercise session. The body's reaction to high altitudes closely mimics its reaction to anesthetics, making the White Mountain Research Station—located 12,000 feet above sea level in the eastern Sierra—an ideal place for the two scientists to conduct fieldwork. Researchers come from around the world to study at the White Mountain Station, which was established by the university in 1950. *Photographer: P.F. Bentley*

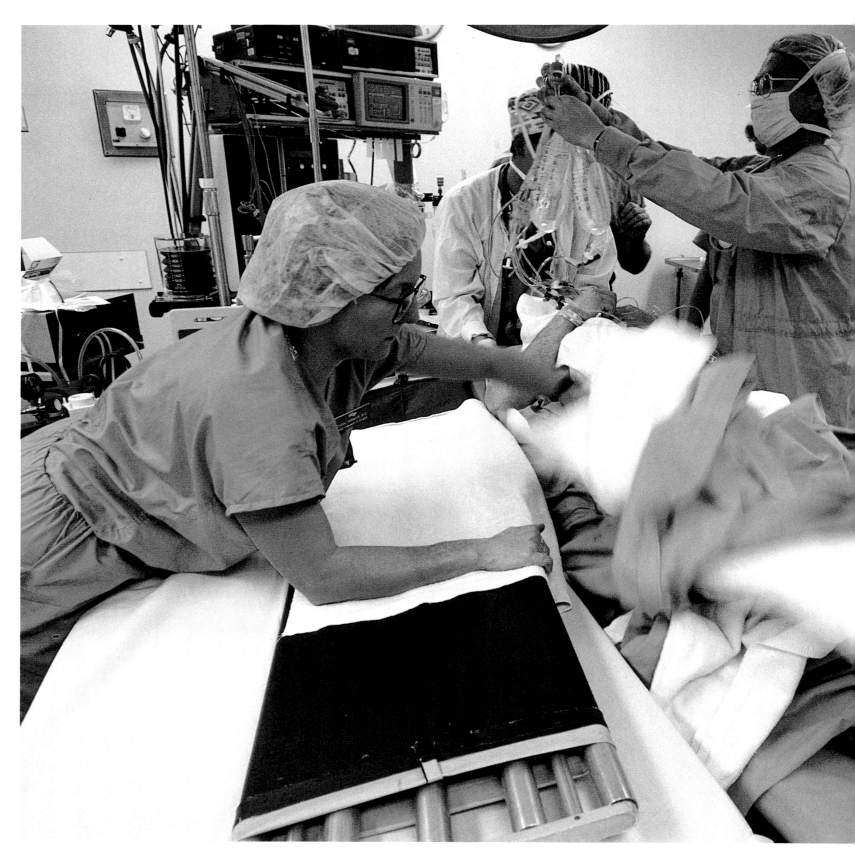

LEFT AND ABOVE: "Surgeons aren't known for their patience," says Diana Farmer. "We want things to happen quickly." The senior resident gets her wish in the trauma center of San Francisco General Hospital's Emergency Department, where she works 24 hours on and 24 hours off during the fifth year of her six-year residency program at UCSF. Like most residents at UCSF, Farmer rotates among several Bay Area hospitals to ensure a wide variety of experiences. The pace is most hectic at San Francisco General, where the emergency room sees about 80,000 patients a year.

Farmer says her feelings each day range "from excitement to terror to satisfaction to disappointment." But in a typical 24-hour shift, she doesn't have much time to dwell on her emotions. "It's a high-energy job," she says, from early-morning rounds to a midday session in the operating room—where she usually serves as primary surgeon—to follow-up rounds late into the night. In between, she consults with other physicians and studies patient charts and X-rays. "The schedule takes a little getting used to," she says, "but it gets better as time goes on. Otherwise, none of us would do it." *Photographer: P.F. Bentley*

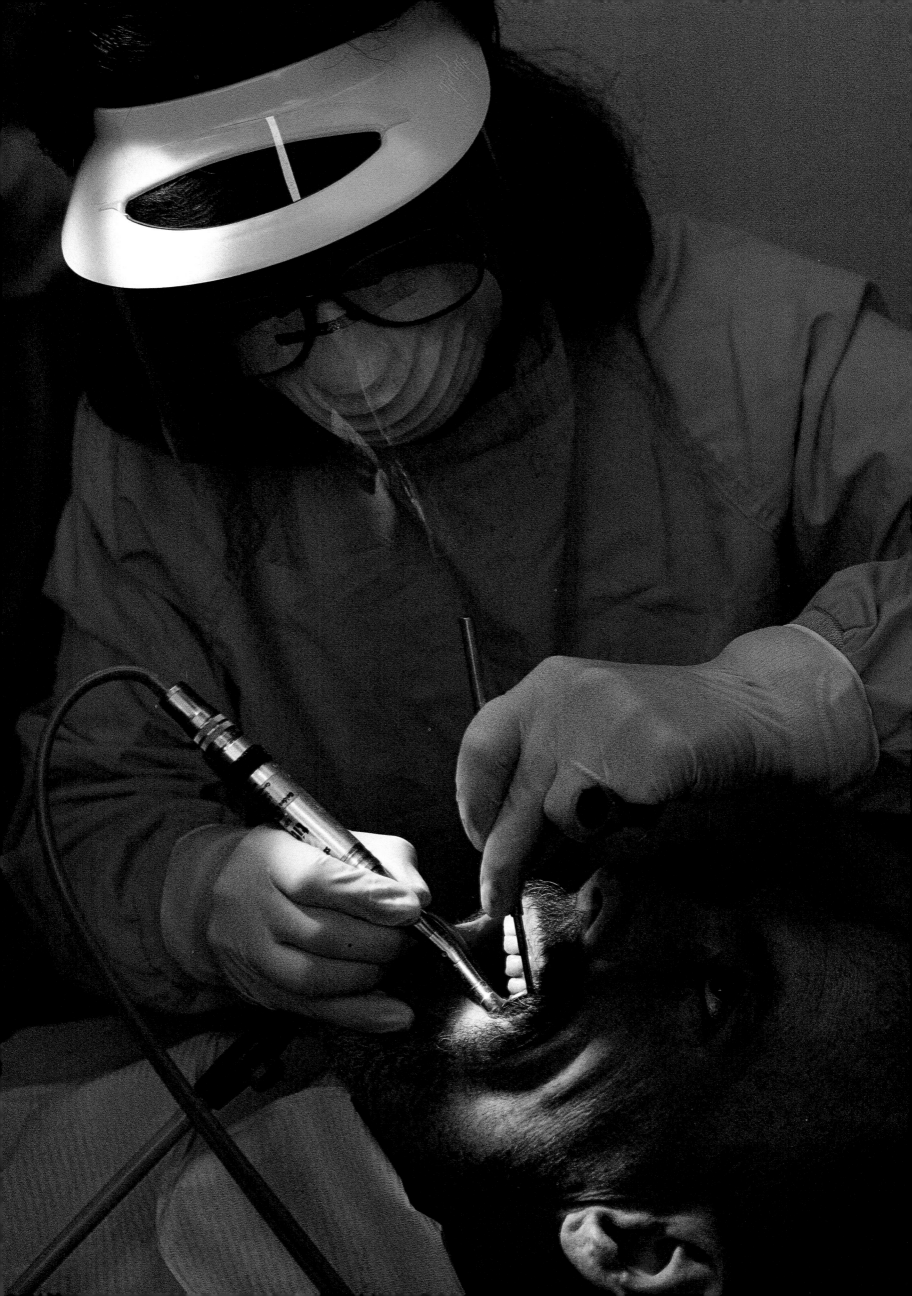

LEFT AND ABOVE: At UCSF, a husband and wife attack the medical scourge of our time. Deborah Greenspan, clinical professor of oral medicine, works on AIDS patients suffering from mouth lesions; later, she confers with her husband John, professor of oral biology and pathology and director of the UCSF Oral AIDS Center. The British-born pair headed a UCSF team that was among the first to describe oral AIDS symptoms in the early 1980s and then began developing treatment for HIV-related oral problems. With their accomplishments, they joined several other scientists—including Marcus Conant, Paul Volberding and Constance Wofsy—who have made the UCSF campus the country's premier AIDS research center. "The cross-fertilization of ideas from doctors, dentists, researchers and pharmacologists makes our work possible," says John Greenspan. Adds Deborah, "Every day on the job is important, because every day someone needs our help." *Photographer: P.F. Bentley*

RIGHT: Associate research immunologist Janet Yamamoto gets a playful hello from a subject in her lab at UC Davis. In 1986, Yamamoto and her collaborator Niels Pedersen discovered the Feline Immunodeficiency Virus, or FIV, the feline counterpart to the AIDS-causing Human Immunodeficiency Virus; in the years since, she has collaborated with scientists around the world in an effort to find a vaccine for FIV. Yamamoto says her primary goal is to "save cats from misery" while making a more general contribution to veterinary medicine. But she adds that, although FIV poses no danger to humans, the 30 cats in her lab offer "a small-animal model for the study of HIV infection." So far, the experimental vaccine Yamamoto is using seems to be effective in warding off FIV infection. *Photographer: Chuck O'Rear*

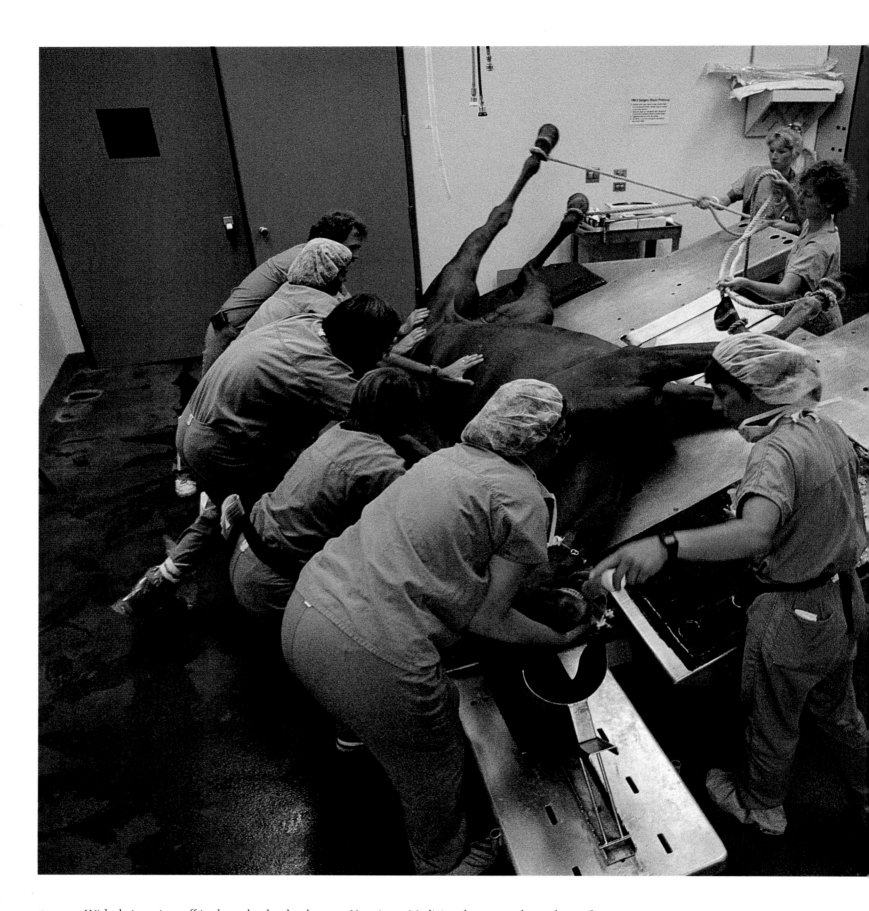

ABOVE: With their patient off in dreamland—thanks to a horse-sized dose of anesthesia—blue-clad veterinary students help five technicians prepare the animal for one of the half-dozen daily horse operations at the Davis Veterinary Center. About 500 students are enrolled at any one time at the vet school, the only one in California and one of only 27 in the country. During the six-year journey toward a Doctor of Veterinary Medicine degree, students choose from such courses as Diseases of Free Living Wildlife, Small Animal Theriogenology and Current Topics in Veterinary Oncology. By the end of the program, they may have operated on animals as diverse as dogs, cats, cows, sheep, goats, pigs, snakes, llamas and even giraffes, which suffer from chronic back problems.
Photographer: Chuck O'Rear

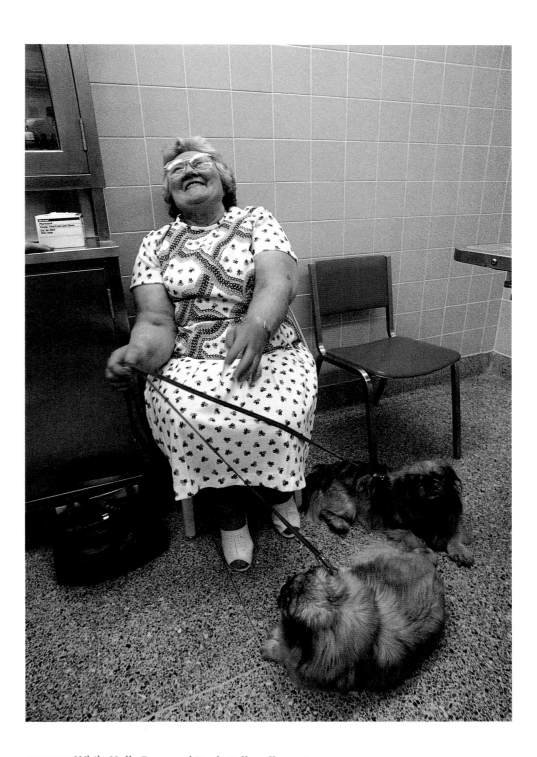

ABOVE: While Holly Berry and Jingle Bell sniff out the surroundings in the waiting room at the vet center on the Davis campus, owner Brenda Sainsbury Cole confesses to some nervousness about the tests the 13-year-old Pekingese dogs are scheduled to take. The vet center offers high-quality health services to pets and farm animals in Davis and outlying communities; it also treats animals from the Sacramento Zoo and animal theme parks in the Bay Area.
Photographer: Chuck O'Rear

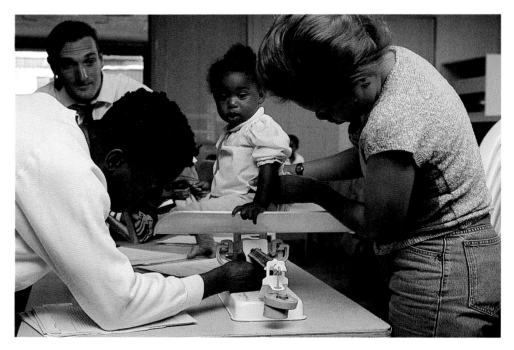

LEFT: Pilar Bernal de Pheils, assistant clinical professor at the UCSF School of Nursing, provides hands-on prenatal care to Silgiau Florez at the Mission Neighborhood Health Center. Bernal de Pheils spends one day a week at the clinic, located in a predominantly Hispanic neighborhood of San Francisco. The School of Nursing has more students than any other department at UCSF, admitting about 350 students each year. *Photographer: P.F. Bentley*

BELOW LEFT: Ten-month-old Sandra Rosa Bryant weighs in at the UCLA/Salvation Army Family Outreach Clinic in West Los Angeles, as second-year medical student Sam Jones checks the scale. Sandra Rosa and her mother Sandra are among 15 families living in a Salvation Army housing village a mile from the UCLA campus; health care for the familes is provided by the Outreach Clinic, run by students at the UCLA School of Medicine, who provide immunizations and other basic medical services. Says David Sanders, one of the students who founded the clinic, "we also talk to patients about personal and dental hygiene, reproductive health, and smoking and substance abuse." Faculty advisor Richard Usatine, assistant professor of family medicine, adds that the clinic experience can't be duplicated in a classroom: "The medical students who created this clinic are learning about medicine while providing kind and compassionate care to a population that's medically underserved." *Photographer: Ricardo DeAratanha*

RIGHT: Doctor-to-be Esther Paek sits for a blood pressure measurement as part of a class in the biomedical sciences program at UC Riverside. Although there is no medical school at Riverside, a joint program with UCLA—the only one of its kind in the state—allows students to complete both their Bachelor of Science and M.D. degrees in seven years rather than the traditional eight. *Photographer: Andy Levin*

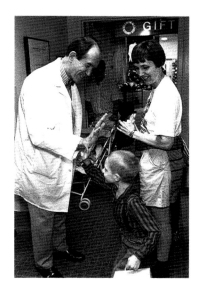

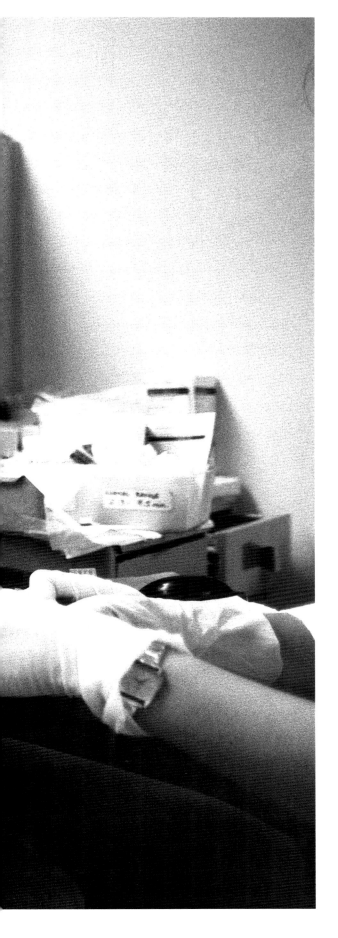

LEFT AND ABOVE: Compared with some of Dr. Warwick Peacock's regular visitors at the Pediatric Neurosurgery Section at the UCLA School of Medicine, who come from as far away as Malaysia, Sweden and Argentina, members of the Hayward family of Wheaton, Illinois, almost seem like neighbors. Peacock, who perfected an operation called a selective posterior rhizotomy—designed to relieve spasticity in children with cerebral palsy—frequently shares his surgical techniques with visiting surgeons from around the world.

Six-year-old Benjamin Hayward, though, has come for the surgery itself, and upon check-in earns a welcoming high-five from Peacock (*top*). Benjamin's not sure the whole thing is such a good idea when a nurse takes blood while he sits in his father's arms, his concerned twin brother Joseph looking on (*left*); later, John and Linda Hayward get some last-minute reassurance from operating-room nurses (*above*) before the surgery begins. "I can't think of anywhere in the world I'd rather be than UCLA," says Peacock, a South Africa native who before coming to UCLA was the only pediatric neurosurgeon on the continent of Africa. "We're learning tremendous amounts about the brain." *Photographer: Mark Wexler*

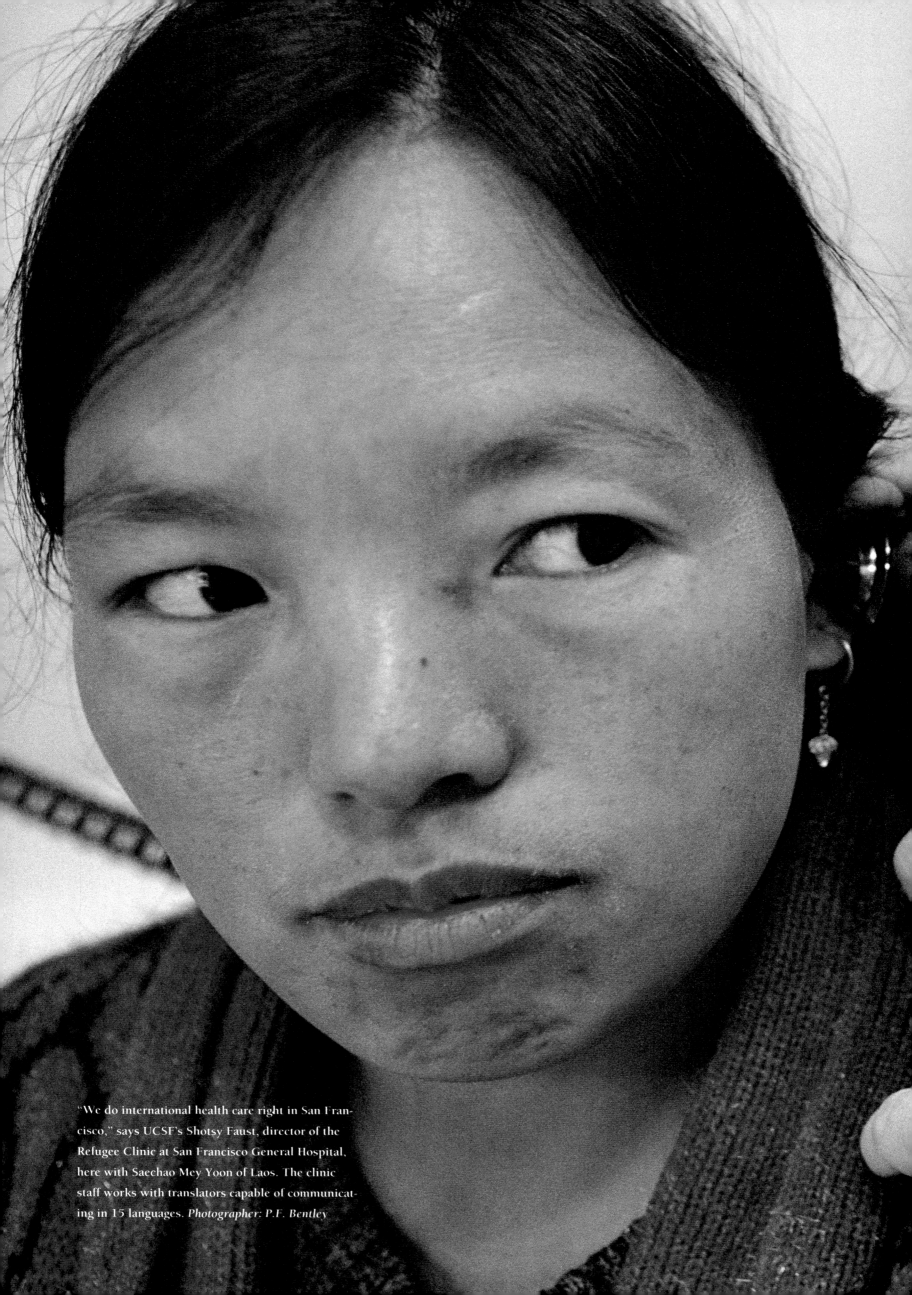

"We do international health care right in San Francisco," says UCSF's Shotsy Faust, director of the Refugee Clinic at San Francisco General Hospital, here with Saechao Mey Yoon of Laos. The clinic staff works with translators capable of communicating in 15 languages. *Photographer: P.F. Bentley*

1. Gov't Freeway + Public
Housing Projects
5. Exclusionary Zoning
Housing Audits
TESTERS

Berkeley

Davis

Irvine

Los Angeles

Riverside

San Diego

San Francisco

Santa Barbara

Santa Cruz

RETHINKING THE IVORY TOWER

A theory gaining currency in recent years suggests an interrelationship between physical, biological, social and economic cycles. For example, arctic-fox abundance in Canada ran exactly in four-year cycles between 1872 and 1931; life-insurance sales in the United States ran in nine-year cycles between 1854 and 1964; and the dominant cycle of civil unrest since 600 B.C. has averaged approximately 25 years.

The "cycle scientists" who track such things believe this cycle of civil unrest may be linked to climatic cycles. "The two appear to be tied well together," noted Richard Mogery of the Foundation for the Study of Cycles, which has no connection with the University of California. "The climate tends to move from warm and wet to cold and dry. This has nothing to do with the Greenhouse Effect, incidentally, or the hole in the ozone layer. Right now we're approaching the end of this cycle, a colder, dryer period, which we expect to peak in about 1997. At the same time, we should see increasing unrest." Mr. Mogery made his comment two months before the acquittals of four white Los Angeles policemen in the beating of a black motorist named Rodney King led to the most extensive civil unrest in America in a century.

Despite its questionable value as a predictor (and above-normal temperatures around the globe), cycle theory expresses a belief among some people, an intuition, that a period of "turmoil and revelation" is in the offing such as we last saw in the 1960s, and in the 1930s before that. The University of California has long been a bellwether of such swings in the public mood. As Verne Stadtman wrote in his definitive history, *The University of California 1868-1968*, "With the onset of the Depression, some students ... became aware by observation if not from personal experience of the existence of poverty and the agonies of chilled spines and empty stomachs. Out of their awareness came a resolve to improve the human condition wherever and as best they could. They found places to start among classmates who were at the mercy of greedy landlords and exploitive employers, or were denied good living accommodations because of their race."

Student concern led to activism on several fronts. At Berkeley, in the spring of 1933, the Social Problems Club protested Japanese imperialism in Manchuria. Later that year, students joined a cotton pickers' strike. There was also a group of pacifists. A handful of "radicals" made enough noise to become noticed, and eventually administrators disallowed these groups to meet or their notices to be displayed.

In the 1960s, of course, there was the Free Speech Movement, which started in the summer of 1964 at Berkeley with a few signup tables to recruit support for the civil rights movement, and culminated at 2:15 p.m. on January 24, 1967, when the Regents voted, 14 to 8, to dismiss University President Clark Kerr. After that, the "rebellion" died down. It had been two-and-a-half years of sit-ins, strikes and strife, and Byzantine political maneuvering on all sides.

For the next 25 years—with two or three exceptions—there was apparent quiet. Yet despite the stillness, questions are being raised in many corners of UC that may be part of that strange breeze in America these days—a breeze blowing out of the grass roots, and from such unexpected directions as David Duke and the Green Party. The questions are both ancient and topical, but foremost among them may be this: In the new puzzle called "multicultural America"—and particularly California—how should the bulwark of Anglo-Saxon culture be adjusted to accommodate ever-larger groups of Asians, blacks, and Hispanics?

The journey to those answers leads in turn to a broader inquiry into the nature of opportunity. Is it opening or closing? Are jobs, health care and education to be considered rights or privileges? As for education, what is the responsibility of a public university in helping those with the fewest opportunities? What are the values and responsibilities that accompany opportunity?

LEFT: At the college level, geography is far more than naming state capitals and locating Burkina Faso on a map. It's also the study of transportation systems, soil use and even—in this seminar about urban landscapes, taught by UCLA professor James Johnson—poverty and public policy. *Photographer: Ricardo DeAratanha*

In the context of an institution like the University of California, the answers are particularly elusive. Each of the nine UC campuses is rooted in a very different community, each facing multicultural fissions, nationwide recession, state budget deficits, even talk of regional secession. Then, for each campus, add increasing numbers of applicants, dwindling resources, a new university presidency, and the traditional struggle between regents and administrators on the one hand, faculty and students on the other, and a thousand variations in between.

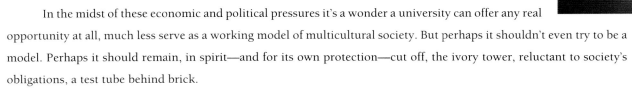

Jim Gensheimer

In the midst of these economic and political pressures it's a wonder a university can offer any real opportunity at all, much less serve as a working model of multicultural society. But perhaps it shouldn't even try to be a model. Perhaps it should remain, in spirit—and for its own protection—cut off, the ivory tower, reluctant to society's obligations, a test tube behind brick.

There's a myth at UC Irvine that the campus was designed to stifle student unrest. The campus is shaped roughly like a broken wagon wheel. Farthest from the center are the dormitories; then, closer in, classrooms; and finally, at the center, a small park with a handful of trees. There is no "yard" in the Harvard sense. "It was built in response to the riots at Berkeley in the 1960s," I was told by an editor at the *New University* newspaper. "They didn't want that to happen here, so they designed a campus with no gathering place for students, no center and very few exits, and they put in underground tunnels so faculty could leave in case of emergency. There are pictures of them somewhere."

Ricardo DeAratanha

Although there are tunnels—built to facilitate equipment delivery—activism-proof architecture was not the idea. It makes a better story, it adds to the legend, but the truth is that the design was conceived in innocence by Clark Kerr. In 1961, three years before the trouble at Berkeley, he sketched out a series of concentric circles on a piece of yellow notebook paper. "Riots were the last thing I was thinking of when I drew that up," replied Dr. Kerr when asked about the design. "That was a period of relative apathy. There was no hint of what was to come."

Dr. Kerr added, "But you know, what you were told makes me think of that scene in *Through the Looking-Glass,* when Alice is looking off down the road and the king asks her if she sees anyone coming. She replies, 'I see nobody.' And the retort is, 'I only wish *I* had such eyes, to be able to see Nobody! And at that distance too!'" Some would say that's the heart of the matter these days at the University of California: students, faculty, administrators, and regents all have their own idea of who Nobody is. The differences in perception are both semantical and philosophical. But in time the consequences may be profound.

Professor Jim Johnson has a clear view of nobodies. He's an urban geographer at UCLA. He studies the demographic lay of the land, the topography of ethnicity. He thinks about distances in terms of how people can travel, in both economic and political terms, from one part of town to another. The town he thinks about most is Los Angeles—where the unemployment rate in some south-central areas runs to 70 percent, where the dropout rate over four years at Loch High School in the same area reached 78 percent in the late 1980s. Where the nobodies are wearing out their invisibility. "L.A. will be to social scientists in the late 20th century what Chicago was in the early 20th century, a quintessential urban laboratory in which to do research on urban issues," says Johnson. "L.A. is on the cutting edge of a series of demographic and economic forces that will eventually transform all U.S. cities. It is a Third World metropolis in which people of color have become the dominant population.

Doug Menuez

"The university cannot be an ivory tower in the midst of an ethnically diverse community, nor can it ignore the pressing social issues of our society. Steps are already being taken to develop stronger ties to the community. But we are not yet on the forefront of dealing with issues that affect the community as a whole. Change is going to demand leadership from inside the university, and some risk-taking."

By some measures, of course, it's becoming increasingly difficult even to differentiate between campus and community. In terms of ethnicity alone, UC is cut very much of the same cloth as the population it serves. UCLA's student body is about one-third Caucasian and one-third Asian. UC San Diego is less than half Caucasian. And in 1991, for the first time, the majority of the entering freshman class at Berkeley was non-white. Other campuses are undergoing similar transformations. In short, UC's student population ranks among the most diverse of any major university in America and, by most accounts, the world.

R obert Bellah occupies an office in UC Berkeley's Barrows Hall, which looks like an apartment building constructed during the Cold War in East Germany. Bellah is a sociologist, co-author of *Habits of the Heart* and *The Good Society*. He's a tall, thin man, sandy-haired, with a bit of whimsy about him. He's also a giant in peace and justice circles, though elsewhere—as he is the first to admit—he is "on the margins" because of his seemingly unscientific method and his criticism of the "research university."

Bellah represents those deep in the lair of the university most critical of the present paradigm: "the disinterested search for the truth." He opposes what he sees as an obsession with the cognitive as opposed to the evaluative, the "is" rather than the "ought"—in sum, the idea that the university's responsibility is to understand how society functions rather than considering how it *ought* to function.

"The dominant ethos today," he says, "is to communicate to students a critical consciousness which can be used to scrutinize and, in a negative sense, call into question all received truths—anything that has been taken for granted in the culture, any ideas that come from home or church or politicians."

The dark view from Bellah's window is of a university faculty who, even within their own discipline, often don't talk to each other; of students who, unlike their counterparts in the 1960s, have no confidence in the future—which includes the worst job market in 30 years; and a student culture which, as Berkeley chaplain Peter Haynes put it several years ago, seems to be "competing for first-class staterooms on the *Titanic*."

Doug Menuez

Bellah and others are calling for a new paradigm in which the university serves as a laboratory for society, a seedbed for ideas and a forum in which public discourse raises consciousness both in the university and in the society. In essence, it is a return to the Greek model, in which the student is assumed to be a citizen of the state from the beginning and is trained to that responsibility.

Bellah's deep pessimism is balanced by what might be described as a strategy of awareness. In *The Good Society*, Bellah and his co-authors argue that "democracy means paying attention." In order to pay attention, one must take responsibility and, above all, trust: "... most people try to limit the scope of their trust. They will trust in this person or this occupation or this ethnic group or this religion or this nation, but not in the other. Yet every such limitation impairs the possibility of responsible action. Since we can only attend to those we trust, we cannot interpret accurately, we cannot be accountable to, we cannot grow in solidarity with those who have been put outside the circle of our trust. This is no abstract argument. On it hinges the very possibility of whether or not we can create something even partially resembling a good society."

Andy Levin

TOP: A protestor's plaintive sign offers a one-word commentary on one of the longest-running political controversies in Berkeley—the fate of People's Park. The university-owned park, a three-acre plot of land three blocks from campus, became a symbol of student protests during the late 1960s and early 1970s. In the summer of 1991, the university succeeded in overcoming blockades by demonstrators and constructed volleyball courts on the site, which had increasingly become a campground for the homeless. *Photographer: Ben Ailes*

ABOVE: Placards in Sproul Plaza at Cal present a historical perspective on the People's Park clash. *Photographer: Doug Menuez*

LEFT: Student demonstrations have been an integral part of the university scene since the landmark Free Speech Movement began at Berkeley in 1964; here, as California Governor Pete Wilson and U.S. Supreme Court Justice Anthony Kennedy dedicate a new building at the UCLA Law School, activists protest the governor's veto of a gay rights bill. *Photographer: Ricardo DeAratanha*

ABOVE: As the university increasingly reflects all the colors of the California rainbow, students find themselves grappling with issues of ethnic identity and race relations. Twenty years ago, the student body of UC was about 80 percent white; now whites comprise less than half the undergraduate students at three campuses (Berkeley, Irvine and UCLA) and about 60 percent of all students in the system. The diversification of the student body is not uniform throughout the university: At Santa Barbara and Santa Cruz, Chicanos and Latinos make up the largest minority group, while Berkeley is home to the highest percentage of African-American students, about 7 percent. The highest percentage of Asians—who account for one in five students throughout the system—is at Irvine, where they comprise about 32 percent. Overall, minority representation, particularly at the undergraduate level, has been rising steadily throughout the last decade. *Photographer: Jim Gensheimer*

ABOVE: Two women stake out positions in Berkeley's Sproul Plaza, the heart and soul of life on campus. Each day, both the impassioned and the curious crowd around the card tables jammed together and staffed by students from some of the 370 on-campus student organizations, including the Ayn Rand Society, Berkeley Students for Choice, the Sikh Student Association and Students That Advocate Accurate Mailing Practices. The on-campus organizations owe their presence at Sproul to the Free Speech Movement, which successfully fought against an attempt by university administrators to keep students from soliciting funds for social and political groups on campus. Elsewhere in the reaches of Sproul, stand-up comedians and jugglers entertain passers-by, street preachers offer a vision of salvation, and students sit on the steps of Sproul Hall to take in the sun, wait for friends or simply watch the best show in town.
Photographer: Doug Menuez

OVERLEAF: In full battle dress for their weekly lab class, third-year cadets in the Reserve Officers Training Corps at UC Davis build on what they've learned of military history, tactics and organization in the classroom. "We train people in leadership," says Captain Alan Villandre, who teaches and advises first-year cadets in the Department of Military Science. "We care about students and we work with them." There are nearly 100 cadets—including 16 women—in the Davis ROTC program, which the ROTC regional brass rates as the best in the western United States. The program pays for books, uniforms and equipment for the cadets, and in some cases offers full scholarships. ROTC programs are also offered at Berkeley, Santa Barbara and UCLA, and students at the other UC campuses can participate through neighboring colleges and universities.
Photographer: Annie Griffiths Belt

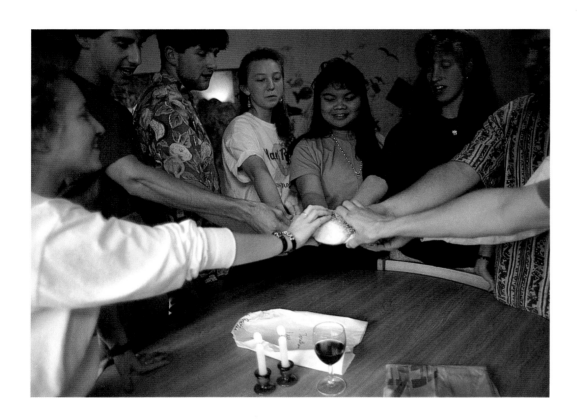

ABOVE: From grief is born a religious community: When a fellow student at Santa Cruz's Stevenson College died three years ago, Jonathan Kupetz and David Feder found they longed for a ritual to help them face their loss. The two began holding informal Shabbat services in their dorm, and now a small group of Jewish students—along with an occasional non-Jewish friend—meets each Friday at sundown to light candles, sing blessings in English and Hebrew and break the special bread known as challah. *Photographer: Jim Gensheimer*

RIGHT: In keeping with the Buddhist belief that nothing is permanent, Tibetan-born Buddhist monk Lobsang Samten, an artist in residence at the University Art Museum in Santa Barbara, leaves behind no physical traces of his brightly colored sand painting. Samten spent five weeks painstakingly forming the six-foot-by-six-foot image, known as a mandala; when completed, the sand painting was blessed, swept into an urn and scattered into the ocean. Samten, a former personal attendant to the Dalai Lama, exiled leader of the Tibetan people, says the purpose of the UCSB mandala was "to reduce attachment, anger and ignorance." *Photographer: Dana Fineman*

TOP: The mood is decidedly young and loud on the airwaves of KALX, Berkeley's campus radio station. Volunteer announcers and disc jockeys—beginners get the 3:30 a.m. to 6:30 a.m. time slot—play at least three distinct kinds of music every hour and also introduce news and public affairs programs.
Photographer: Andy Levin

ABOVE: Election posters dominate a bulletin board at Berkeley, where students vote each year for 15 Associated Students of the University of California senators and five executive officers. Some of the campus political parties—including the Stanford Party, the Politically Educated Non-Interested Students Party and the A Snowball's Chance in Hell that I'll Get Elected Party—attract chuckles as well as voters; others, such as Cal-SERVE (Students for Equal Rights and a Valid Education), are major political organizations, jockeying for control of the ASUC's $18 million annual operating budget. About one in four Cal students votes in a typical campus election.
Photographer: Andy Levin

Berkeley

Davis

Irvine

Los Angeles

Riverside

San Diego

San Francisco

Santa Barbara

Santa Cruz

THE CREATIVE ENCOUNTER

The bookstore owner couldn't think of any recent books on creativity, but, yes, he did know Rollo May's book, *The Courage to Create*. There was one copy, he thought, up on the second floor, in "Used Psychology." And sure enough, just a few books down from *The Act of Creation* by Arthur Koestler, there was Dr. May's book, first published in 1975. It was in good condition, but with a lot of underlining and, in two places, notes in the margin. In one place, Dr. May, a psychiatrist, was relating the view of a contemporary poet that rage—rage against social injustice—ignites the poet's passion. May added, "But ultimately, it is rage against the prototype of all injustice—death."

In the margin was written, very neatly, "Bull! For you, maybe."

The careful script, and the comma after "you," suggested restraint, and perhaps self-consciousness—as though the passion of the response were cut with a sense that this was a book, after all, a permanent document, where this disagreement might one day be read by a stranger.

In another section, Dr. May, a former Regents' Professor at UC Santa Cruz, writes that creativity is not an expression of neurosis—the psychological struggles of such great artists as Van Gogh, Gauguin and Virginia Woolf notwithstanding. In the margin was written, again very neatly, in pen: "Creativity is a passion; and scientists may not like to confront passions—their own or those of others."

It was a non sequitur to what May was talking about, suggesting that perhaps the reader was herself or himself a scientist, a young biology or chemistry student, feeling inhibited by the rigors of Scientific Method and disappointed that passion, intuition and creativity seemed to have no place in the laboratory.

The idea of a frustrated chemistry student brings to mind Donald Cram, a professor emeritus of chemistry who has taught for 44 years at UCLA. He is a lanky man with boyish blue eyes who still surfs at the age of 78. Last winter he broke a rib skiing.

Dr. Cram comes from a pinprick of a town in Vermont, where he grew up mostly in his mother's boarding house. He was the fourth of five children. When he was four, his father died. His father had once been a cavalry officer. As a child, Cram was entranced by the romantic heroes he read about in Tennyson, Kipling, and Sir Walter Scott. Later he found a comparable romanticism, and nobility, in organic chemistry. As a scientist, Dr. Cram imagined himself as one of the 600 riding down into Tennyson's Valley of Death—down into the subatomic world of molecules, sometimes charging against nature itself.

But for many years Dr. Cram did not fully realize his hero's dream. He was devoted to his work, forever devising new molecular shapes. He thought of himself as more an artist than a scientist. He took great pride in his creativity, and intuition, and became known for the innovative shapes of his molecules. His designs gradually took on a "signature."

And all the while Dr. Cram put his art, and his science, before everything else. He had no children just to avoid the distraction.

After 25 years of marriage he got a divorce which, he realized with great sadness at the time, was partly the result of his work on other chemistries. But after a time he met another woman, and perhaps by coincidence he set out on a slightly different track in his work. It was then, in the liberating moments of this new relationship, that he had a revelation about a complementary way in which molecules could be made to fit together. For his creativeness, and for leading the team that gave birth to his idea, Dr. Cram won the Nobel Prize in 1987.

LEFT: The Picassos of the future still need reminders about studio etiquette at Davis, home to one of the country's leading art departments. The department counts among its faculty noted artists Robert Arneson, Roy DeForest, Manuel Neri and Wayne Thiebaud.
Photographer: Annie Griffiths Belt

But his most recent work offers perhaps the best measure of his creative instincts. A few years ago he began to make molecules shaped like containers, into which other molecules can be placed. He calls the container the "host" molecule and the molecule inside the "guest" molecule. His container designs resemble the finest crystal vases. From the containers he got the idea of spheres—a revolutionary idea that makes it possible, for example, to enclose a molecule of lithium and send it through a membrane to an otherwise inaccessible part of the brain.

Jim Mendenhall

"My religion is my profession," Dr. Cram confided recently, sitting in the silence of his "writing" home in the desert east of Los Angeles. "It is not spiritual, it is intellectual, but also intuitive—and artistic."

As Rollo May wrote, "Creativity is the encounter of the intensively conscious human being with his or her world." That's as simple and broad a definition as any—and part of a very modern view that first, creativity is not the private reserve of the artist in the garret; and second, a sculptured molecule, though displayed in only the most exclusive galleries, can be as artistic, and possess as much moral significance, as, say, Van Gogh's *Starry Night*.

Dr. May believed that creativity is a sign of emotional health. Otherwise, one could not be "intensively conscious" and therefore open to the unconscious, that great treasure chest into which the true artist can look, find some new thing, and bring it out into the light. By extension, the healthier the society, the more creativity flourishes. To find true illness, one need only look at Hitler's plans for the dream capital of the Third Reich. Hitler's joy was in that awesome, but terrifying, sense of proportion in which colossal office buildings dominate humanity.

Whatever else one may criticize in America these days, it is still true that all the artistic themes of the day can be seen and heard, for better and for worse. And nowhere is that more true than in the universities. For its part, the University of California has long been a center of artistic inquiry. In the 1930s, such talents as Ernst Bloch, Arnold Schoenberg and Roger Sessions taught music, Hans Hoffman painting. In the 1960s, the Institute of Ethnic Arts at UCLA became noted for

Annie Griffiths Belt

its gifted ethnic musicians; drummers from Ghana, musicians from Japan and dancers from Bali all taught courses. In the last 20 years, one thinks of such painters as Wayne Thiebaud, William T. Wiley, Pete Wilkens and Roy DeForest, sculptor Manuel Neri, ceramicist Robert Arneson—all teachers at UC Davis—and Joan Brown at Berkeley. Other well-known artists of recent years include composer Roger Boreland, dance teachers Judy Mitoma and Susan Foster, and performance artists Eleanor Antin at UC San Diego and Chris Burden at UCLA. Writers include Maxine Hong Kingston, Czeslaw Milosz, Ishmael Reed, Paula Gun Allen, and Bharati Mukerjee. From UCLA's film school have emerged director Francis Ford Coppola, screen actress Carol Burnett, stage actress Joanna Kearns, and screenwriters Colin Higgins, Shane Black and Neil Jiminez. Jim Morrison graduated from UCLA. James Dean and Rob Reiner attended as well.

All these artists, their works and their teaching define a timeline of creativity in the 20th century. The timeline suggests not only evolutions of thought within each art, but also a trend toward multicultural influences and expression—and a growing syncretism of art and technology.

"The greatest change in art at the end of the 20th century," says UCLA art department chairman Henry Hopkins, "is that ideas are moving so quickly now. Periods don't last. In the past, a movement like Impressionism would run its course until it exhausted itself. Now a period or phase is condensed. If an artist does something interesting, the idea is accessible right away. Within weeks other artists are imitating and improvising and going off in other directions. The dark side in this is that creativity may burn out more quickly because it's being consumed so quickly. An artist has a much more difficult time keeping himself viable. But on the other side, accessibility enriches creativity, growth and innovation."

If there were a word to describe this period, in the way Rationalism and Romanticism once did theirs, perhaps it would be "Wholism." In essence, to risk a generalization, the prevailing trend in the arts is toward ever more inclusiveness—stylistically, culturally and technologically. The enlightened art is that which suggests an overarching unity, and leads the viewer to experience that as a sensation.

I n the current critical climate, the quality of a piece is more a matter of purpose than performance. The goal is not beauty so much as "what works." In the 1990s, in fact, it often seems to be the faculty more than the students who are pressing for freedom of expression, at least "inner expression." Technique is secondary.

"I've never trusted art history," says UC Davis sculptor Lucy Puls, "I suppose because women artists are so rarely mentioned. But I do trust the history of science—that's something I've always been interested in—and it seems to me that accidents and mistakes are often at the heart of scientific breakthroughs. That process is one of the keys to creativity. I try to teach my students to pay attention to the process of making their work—and if they make a mistake during the process, then perhaps that's significant. And maybe the mistake should be left in because it reveals something about the truth you started with, that you're trying to discover."

"What we're trying to offer," says Judy Mitoma, chairman of the UCLA dance department, "is the emotional dimension of creativity by concentrating on process. It is through process, and being evaluated, that one experiences tension and self-doubt. But it is in that moment of taking a risk that

P.F. Bentley

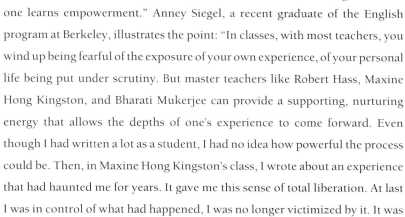

one learns empowerment." Anney Siegel, a recent graduate of the English program at Berkeley, illustrates the point: "In classes, with most teachers, you wind up being fearful of the exposure of your own experience, of your personal life being put under scrutiny. But master teachers like Robert Hass, Maxine Hong Kingston, and Bharati Mukerjee can provide a supporting, nurturing energy that allows the depths of one's experience to come forward. Even though I had written a lot as a student, I had no idea how powerful the process could be. Then, in Maxine Hong Kingston's class, I wrote about an experience that had haunted me for years. It gave me this sense of total liberation. At last I was in control of what had happened, I was no longer victimized by it. It was

Jim Gensheimer

a powerful, cathartic experience. Now I constantly feel the weight of these internal experiences, their intensity. I'm thinking of going on in creative writing. I mean, when I came to UC, I was going to be a marine-mammal vet."

Not all are so fortunate. In the view of numerous arts faculty, many of today's students languish in a kind of cultural wallow, at once stultified by television and overstimulated by the train-wreck collision of science and pop culture. Many experience difficulty in finding their own voices, their own values. "They're much different now than when I started teaching eight years ago," says Squeak Carnwath, a painter who has taught at both Berkeley and Davis. "Students are much more worried about what people think of their work these days, particularly beginning students. They take fewer risks. They ask fewer questions. And different questions. They want to know the 'correct' answers, they want somebody to tell them how to proceed. When I started, students seemed to be more interested in seeing how it worked. How to get paint

to work in a certain way. They were more technique-oriented. Now, older students are more interested in the gallery system. 'How do I sell my work?' Marketing the end product, not the process. They're also much more mimetic: they want to replicate what they think they see, not what they feel."

To Jim Clifford, an anthropologist at UC Santa Cruz, such gloomy assessments overlook the obvious: that times have changed. "I'm skeptical when I hear how students have been damaged by television and popular culture," he says. "It's true that students now don't read in the way they did before. But they're visually literate, and they don't

Mark Wexler

think the way they did before. We're going from inspiration and genius to innovativeness and the ability to adapt. We often read that as decline rather than difference. But much of what we're seeing now is the result of cultural diversity. You look out on a classroom now and it is *different*. I have an African-American grad student who recently taught *The Tempest* using a Madonna video. It was an excellent class. He got the students to see how interesting problems of race could be. If you go with traditional notions of literacy, you may be missing one of the most powerful avenues into critical consciousness."

LEFT: Santa Cruz student actors Lisa Worthey, Christopher Sebastian, Craig Souza and *(rear)* Susannah Schulman take to the stage in Bertolt Brecht's *The Good Woman of Setzuan*, in a production lauded by critics as a "visual treat" with a "conscientious and consistent" cast. Theater arts majors at Santa Cruz choose classes in four areas of concentration—drama, theater design and technology, dance, and film and video—and are required to study theater history and theory as well as to strut their stuff on the boards. The most comprehensive theater program in the system is found at UC Berkeley. *Photographer: Jim Gensheimer*

RIGHT: While the atmosphere during most final exams is deadly serious, Suzan Hughes' best chance for an "A" is a roomful of laughter. Like the other 25 students in the Performing Stand-Up Comedy class offered by UCLA Extension's Performing and Integrated Arts Program, Hughes takes her final by taking to the stage, performing a stand-up routine in front of a live audience at The Improvisation, a comedy club in Santa Monica. "I love stand-up," says Hughes. "You're the writer, producer, director and actor all at once, so if it bombs you have no one to blame but yourself—and if it goes well, you get all the credit." As at the other general-education UC campuses, extension classes at UCLA primarily serve adult students who are not enrolled in the university. At UCLA alone, more than 4,000 extension classes are offered each year in subjects ranging from accounting to celestial navigation, and more than 100,000 individuals sign up to take advantage of this bridge between the university and the residents of Los Angeles. *Photographer: Jim Mendenhall*

RIGHT: A research assistant checks the canisters in the Film and Television Archive at UCLA as part of the archive's program to preserve works of high art and low for future generations. The archive includes more than 200,000 feature films, newsreels, short programs and television shows; much of the material, preserved on nitrate film and dating back as far as the 1890s, is in danger of literally turning to dust unless it is converted to safety film in the next several years. Public and private funds help the archive finance the transfers to safety film, which can cost as much as $25,000 per film. *Photographer: Mark Wexler*

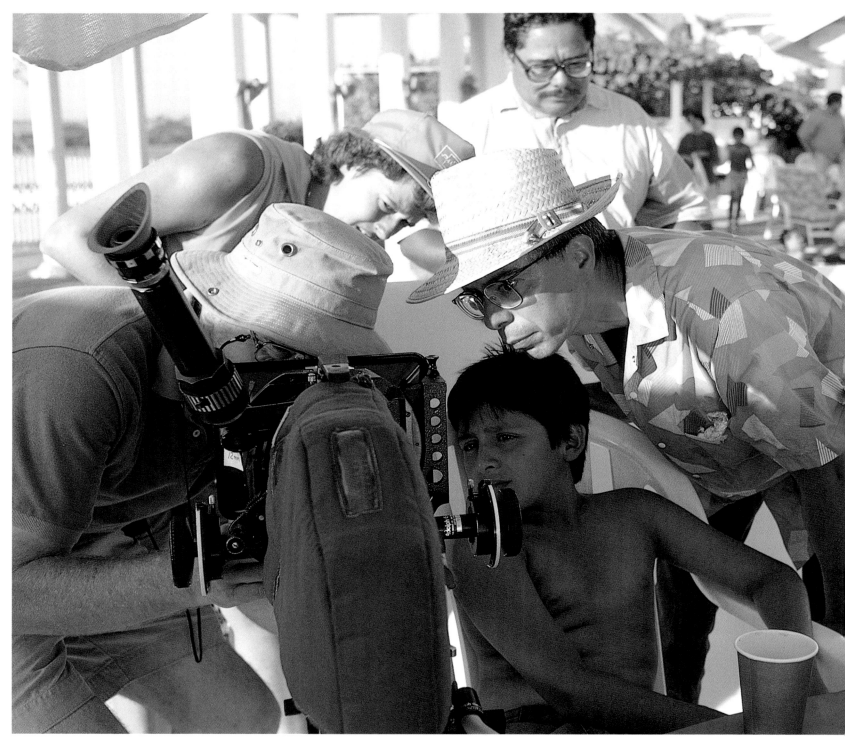

ABOVE: Kelly Lynn Wilbur pushes a television and videocassette recorder up an incline as part of the delivery service offered by Riverside's Media Resources Department. *Photographer: Andy Levin*

LEFT: Translating his vision from the printed page to the small screen, Berkeley's Gary Soto leans over to check a shot for the half-hour comedy film *The Pool Party*. Soto, who earned his Master's degree from Irvine in 1976, has taught at Cal since 1979 in the English and Chicano Studies departments; along the way, his 16 volumes of poetry and prose have earned him numerous awards. *The Pool Party*, funded in part by UC Mexus—a university-wide consortium devoted to relations between the United States and its neighbor to the south—"is a chance," says Soto, "to extend the lives of Mexican-Americans to television, where their stories are not usually told." *Photographer: Jim Gensheimer*

Professor Philip Collins, a noted Dickens scholar from Britain's University of Leicester, performs a passage from *Pickwick Papers* at the Dickens Universe Project, an annual summer conference at UC Santa Cruz. *Photographer: Jim Gensheimer*

Art students at UC Davis learn from a master: Famed California figurative artist and longtime Davis instructor Wayne Thiebaud works on a charcoal sketch in his Life Drawing class. *Photographer: Annie Griffiths Belt*

Poet and essayist Ishmael Reed urges on a group of poetry students at Berkeley. Reed's Before Columbus Foundation has been a powerful voice promoting multicultural literature. *Photographer: Doug Menuez*

At UC Santa Barbara's six-week Summer Vocal Institute, music professor and institute director Elizabeth Mannion works on technique with Anne Knoche. *Photographer: Jim Mendenhall*

TOP: "I love what I do," says smiling Santa Cruz assistant music professor Nicole Paiement as she rehearses with the UCSC Chamber Singers. The singers are chosen on the basis of campus-wide tryouts and earn two units per quarter for their six hours a week of rehearsals and recitals. *Photographer: Jim Gensheimer*

ABOVE: Suenobu Togi plays the traditional instrument known as a *kakko* as he leads a class in UCLA's Department of Ethnomusicology and Systematic Musicology. Students pursuing a degree in ethnomusicology choose from a wide range of courses, including Afro-American Musical Heritage, Folk Music of the Mediterranean and Togi's Studies in Japanese Court Music. *Photographer: Mark Wexler*

LEFT: The best electric guitar may be an unplugged guitar in Isla Vista, where nearly half of UC Santa Barbara's 18,000 students live. In response to complaints from residents, in 1990 the county Board of Supervisors made it illegal to produce "any loud and unreasonable sound" between 10 p.m. and 7 a.m. on weekdays and midnight and 7 a.m. on weekends. *Photographer: Andy Levin*

ABOVE: Two revelers share a laugh at Santa Cruz's Merrill College Dining Hall during the annual Coming Out Day dance, sponsored by the UCSC Gay, Lesbian and Bisexual Network. *Photographer: Jim Gensheimer*

LEFT: Just another enchanted evening on Berkeley's Fraternity Row, where the brothers of Delta Sigma Phi sponsor their annual Sailors Ball—in which they dress up as Navy men or pirates and their dates come as mermaids or women of the South Pacific. More than 3,000 students belong to Cal's 44 fraternities and 14 sororities. *Photographer: Doug Menuez*

RIGHT: It's a vision of perpetual motion at the Dance Studio at Berkeley. The jewel of UC's dance program is found at Riverside, soon to be home to the country's only doctoral program in dance history and theory. *Photographer: Jim Sugar*

"I'm delighted to take part in their creativity," says UCSB sculpture instructor Collin Gray of the students in his Independent Study in Sculpture course. Gray meets with each student every week to offer critiques; part of his mission, he says, is to "help sculptors find their voice." *Photographer: Andy Levin*

Berkeley

Davis

Irvine

Los Angeles

Riverside

San Diego

San Francisco

Santa Barbara

Santa Cruz

ENGINEERING THE FUTURE

One of the most terrifying incidents of the 1989 Loma Prieta earthquake took place in the Marina District of San Francisco, where a woman had been pinned in her apartment by a fallen beam. The man with whom she was living tried desperately to get the beam off, but couldn't. Meanwhile, fire began moving through the building, an old wooden four-story structure partly collapsed, as though down on its knees. The man shouted for help. People out in the street yelled to him to get out. The fire was getting closer. Aftershocks rattled the building. By the time the fire department arrived, the fire had reached the apartment door. The man jumped out the window into the street to direct firefighters, but then suddenly it was too late. The fire ate everything. It was all they could do to keep the man from going back. He kept screaming again and again, "I can't reach you. I can't reach you. Oh, God, I can't reach you."

Three years later, nothing has changed. There are hardly any "For Rent" signs in the Marina District. The basic problem remains of buildings built on sand and, worse, landfill. And there are still structural problems because of ill-supported garage space on the ground floors of many apartment buildings. But of course people have forgotten. The theology that "it won't happen to me" is as strong as ever.

It's fitting that California should be susceptible to earthquakes. The greater the opportunity, wealth, and beauty, the greater the risk to attain those things. Only in such a larger-than-life place would people endure the prospect of unexpected catastrophe, and on a huge scale. You might think the automobile would be the logical nemesis for Californians. Almost 5,000 people die in car accidents in California every year—more than have died from earthquakes in the state in the last 90 years. Yet it's the earthquake that seems to stick in the psyche. That's the true dragon in the fairy tale called California.

But if it's our worst fear, why do we take such an uneven interest, from an engineering as well as a personal point of view? As one civil engineer at the University of California notes, "There's never been a consistent approach to the problem. Why not? Ask the politicians. They've never been able to sustain the political will to keep the funding going. Research always goes in fits and starts. It follows a crisis. Even now our facilities are not being used as much as they might be. ... That's one reason we're always behind. Another is that we're always fighting the next earthquake with knowledge we had two earthquakes ago."

After the "big one" in 1906, the area destroyed by fire was regarded by builders as a blank slate on which to try out new designs. A great deal of knowledge about earthquake engineering was available, both from that quake and from previous ones around the world, but that knowledge was largely ignored. According to an engineering report written in 1984, the 11,000 unreinforced masonry buildings in San Francisco, most of them built after 1906, show little attention to construction details that can prevent collapse in a major shock. It wasn't until 1947 that seismic regulations were adopted in San Francisco.

A variety of earthquake research got under way at the University of California as early as 1872, following a major temblor in the Owens Valley. In 1887, it was Edward S. Holden, head of the University of California's Lick Observatory—and for a brief time the reluctant president of UC—who installed the first seismographs in the United States, at the observatory and at the Berkeley campus, and began to produce an annual list of earthquakes on the West Coast.

LEFT: Stronger than steel, lighter than aluminum and baked in a furnace at 1,500 degrees Fahrenheit, cermet—short for ceramic metal—is among the latest innovations at the Lawrence Livermore National Laboratory, one of three national laboratories administered by the university. *Photographer: P.F. Bentley*

A century later, major earthquake research continues at several campuses, including Berkeley, San Diego, Irvine, Riverside and Davis. Structural engineers throughout the UC system remain under contract with Caltrans, which oversees the state's freeway system as well as some 11,000 bridges. Engineers are developing quake-resistant building designs; new construction materials; and a variety of retrofit mechanisms. Plans exist to put buildings on "skates," actually a system of elastomeric bearings that would allow a structure to slide back and forth slightly at its base. Another innovation calls for enormous coils to hang from bridges and absorb ground motion.

Jim Mendenhall

In addition, two professors from the structural engineering department at UC Berkeley—along with other UC graduates—were among the 10-member Governor's Board of Inquiry on the 1989 Loma Prieta Earthquake. The board issued a report in 1990 entitled "Competing Against Time," one of the most comprehensive documents of its kind ever written.

"As a result of this report," says engineering professor Alexander Scordelis of UC Berkeley, a member of the board of inquiry, "the governor, Caltrans, the Golden Gate Bridge District and almost every agency has taken action to improve the situation. The response has been extraordinary."

But the question remains, how much response is needed? And how much can we afford? "What we're finding," says Robert Kazanjy, a senior development engineer in the department of civil engineering at UC Irvine, "is that a lot of these bridges and approaches like the Cypress Viaduct were designed in the '40s and built in the '50s. The design standards are much different now. That doesn't mean that they're necessarily unsafe. In fact, we're finding that most of these structures are much stronger than they would appear. But demand now may be becoming greater than capacity— demand based not merely on the size of the earthquake but on many other factors as well, such as soil change and stress. We've got to evaluate these structures to know what the true demand is.

P.F. Bentley

"You see, the problem with structures, unlike, say, cars, is that they last such a long time. So you're always faced with that problem: should I tear it down, or retrofit? Or look at it this way: sixty-two people died in Loma Prieta. How much money do we need to spend to save that number of people? We would gladly spend $1 million, or $10 million. But would we spend $100 million or $1 billion? If a politician is faced with putting that money toward repairing the infrastructure or AIDS research or creating new jobs, what will be the choice?"

There was a time when civil engineering seemed a glamorous profession, when the construction of roads, dams, and bridges ranked among our top priorities as a people. Today that work continues, but the glamor has moved on. Now it belongs to the likes of the biomedical engineers at UC Santa Barbara who are working to develop optical-radiation diagnostic tools for use in fighting cancer; to the engineers at UC Berkeley who are designing technologies that will one day almost completely automate driving; to the engineers at Lawrence Berkeley Laboratory who are developing sources of ultrabright X-ray and ultraviolet radiation that offer researchers in many fields a new way to study matter. Engineers at Lawrence Livermore National Laboratory make the news regularly with the introduction of one new material after another: the superinsulating aerogels, also known as "frozen smoke"; superplastic steel; piezoelectric materials; and cermets, ceramic-metal alloys lighter than aluminum yet as tough as diamonds.

If the engineering of concrete and asphalt isn't as dramatic as some sister disciplines, nevertheless it is directly tied to infrastructure and the environment, which seem likely to persist—along with education and health care—as the bedrock issues of the 1990s. But those seeking to do meaningful work in this arena face serious obstacles. First, universities themselves are strapped for funds.

P.F. Bentley

Administrative costs and overhead in general have skyrocketed, with as much as 40 percent of grant monies being devoured by such expenses. Second, funding for cutting-edge research, from both public and private sources, tends to follow the glamor, and the promise of saleable products. One of the greatest feats in engineering, at least in academia, comes in returning sufficient value to underwriters while making significant discoveries accessible to all.

The professional orientation of engineering schools in America comes as a mixed blessing. Clearly, developing close relationships with clients in industry is essential for many university engineers if they expect to do any relevant work. But many of them feel mistrusted by faculty from the "core" departments, suspected of being in the pockets of corporate sponsors. And from the other direction come the pressures of underwriters, who prefer to maintain proprietary and secret arrangements in acquiring knowledge.

One place where the relationship between the university and the private sector is working very well—indeed it's a model—is in the Combustion Laboratory at UC Irvine. Professor Scott Samuelsen, director of the laboratory and a professor of mechanical and environmental engineering, has begun a novel effort to try to bridge the gap between opposed interests. His results in this regard may be even more important than the tangible research that comes out of his laboratory.

Some of the lab's research involves finding ways to reduce ozone-depleting emissions from new High-Speed Civil Transports—the big rigs of the stratosphere for the 21st century. Samuelsen, who worked at DuPont and SRI International

Dana Fineman

among other companies before coming to UC, is a strong advocate of using science to protect the environment. He believes that environmentally-sensitive technology need not be more expensive than conventional alternatives, and that those countries that possess such technology will be economic leaders in the future.

"I think the predilection of universities in general," he says, "is to seek isolation rather than incorporation. There's the view that applied research is not as important as basic research. But we need to appreciate that it is equally important to understand how basic mechanisms work in nature and how they work in practical applications. The university review system often treats application as less significant, which comes from a fear of industry on the part of faculty, and because they think it's self-serving."

Dr. Samuelsen's program stresses both basic and applied research and maintains a rigorous integrity in dealings with the private sector. "I can think of two examples where we have ended a relationship with a company because it was not willing to abide by our rules. In one case an industry wished that whatever results we came up with be protected and that publication be limited. This came up six months after our relationship began. We refused and they went somewhere else. That's one of the things that the private sector must understand—the true function of a university." In fact, its enormous intellectual integrity is one of the greatest assets the University of California possesses. In recent years, its strength has been bolstered even further by an array of procedures and reviews designed to prevent conflicts of interest and the temptation of personal financial gain.

P.F. Bentley

Dr. Samuelsen is encouraged by the results of his work in bringing cap and gown and hardhat together. But while hopeful, he is not optimistic about the prospects of the establishment of an industrial policy in the U.S. that would, as it does in Japan, provide a pool of funds—essentially through a tax on industry—that could be used to pay for research in general and graduate work in particular. "There would be several advantages for both the private sector and the university," says Samuelsen. "This kind of policy would allow the university to continue in basic research, which often leads to technical application. More important, it would insure that students are educated to go into these industries. Right now, we're having fewer and fewer students go to graduate school. There's been a tremendous reduction in research overall. I don't think the federal government has any idea that we are losing the technical base we need for the future. It's a win-win situation, if only the blinders could be lifted."

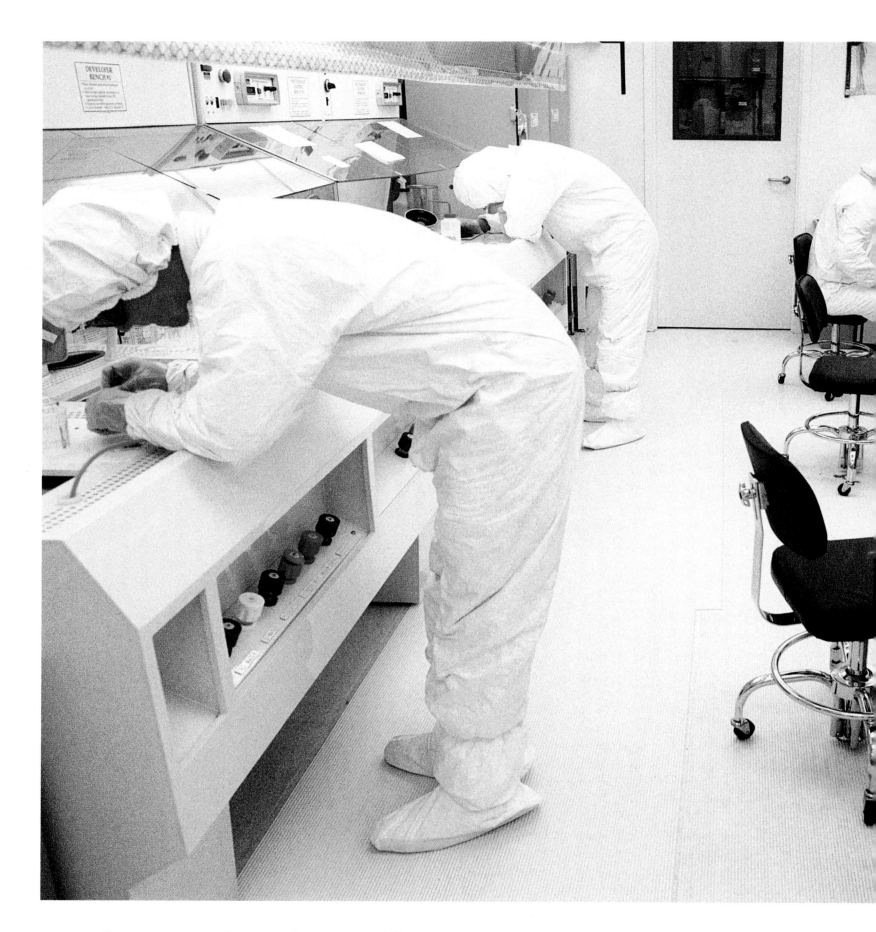

ABOVE: College may mean messy dorm rooms for some, but it means as clean an environment as possible for others—especially these graduate students in electrical engineering at Santa Barbara, working in a chamber known as a clean room at the Center for Quantized Electronic Structures, or QUEST. Researchers use the clean room to work with semiconductors, optical fibers and electron beams in search of electronic structures that could rival the transistor or integrated circuit in their capacity to transform modern life. Although most students will find work as professional researchers, some, says QUEST engineer Jack Wahley, "will open their own companies and become millionaires." *Photographer: Andy Levin*

ABOVE: Where there's smoke, there's ARAC: Scientists with the Atmospheric Release Advisory Capability team at Lawrence Livermore National Laboratory use computer images to trace ash and smoke from the eruption of Mt. Pinatubo in the Philippines. The ARAC team, which used its skills to calculate the extent and magnitude of the radioactive plume from the 1986 Chernobyl nuclear disaster and the smoke from burning oil wells during the Persian Gulf War, was originally put together to predict the dispersion of radioactivity resulting from the detonation of a nuclear bomb or a nuclear weapons accident. Like other groups at the three UC-administered Department of Energy labs, however, it is increasingly branching out into non-defense-related scientific pursuits, including research on laser energy, new materials and the environmental sciences. At Lawrence Livermore Lab, the portion of funding devoted to civilian projects now totals 38 percent. *Photographer: P.F. Bentley*

TOP: As a camera captures the images of cars approaching an intersection in nearby Anaheim, doctoral student John Leonard at Irvine's Institute of Transportation Studies watches the flow of traffic by computer. In a study with obvious implications for California's future, Leonard and other scholars are evaluating the use of advanced technology in traffic control. *Photographer: Laurel Hungerford*

ABOVE: Graduate student Lori Kosakura puts the finishing touches on a project for her Master's degree at UCLA's College of Architecture and Urban Planning. In recognition of Los Angeles' emergence as a new kind of urban environment, UCLA recently established a Center for Regional Policy Studies to research environmental, social-policy and urban-design issues. *Photographer: Jim Mendenhall*

LEFT: It may be an oasis of green, but the Berkeley campus, foreground—featuring the landmark Campanile, designed to resemble that of St. Mark's Square in Venice—is inseparable from the urban environment of the East Bay. Research and other activities at the 1,232-acre campus affect the lives of Californians living far beyond the area the eye can see, which includes downtown Oakland and Lake Merritt in the background. *Photographer: Jim Sugar*

ABOVE: It's not every day that a professor of mechanical engineering makes news, so Berkeley's Kent Udell takes advantage of his moment in the spotlight to explain to reporters his invention: a steam-cleaning machine that treats contaminated soil and groundwater. "Steam cleaning is much cheaper than removing the soil and shipping it to a toxic waste dump," says Udell, adding that the waste flushed out by the steam is concentrated enough to be recycled. Udell's invention may qualify for further development money from Superfund, the federally sponsored environmental clean-up program; even without Udell's contribution, Cal receives more Superfund money than any other research institution in the country.
Photographer: Chris Maynard

LEFT: With an oil rig and the Santa Barbara coast providing the backdrop, Don Konestrow examines a sea urchin specimen with his assistant, marine biology graduate student Ari Martinez. Konestrow, the field director for the Coastal Toxicology Program at UCSB, regularly tests the water and living organisms in the Santa Barbara Channel in an effort to monitor how the presence of human-made structures affects the channel's ecological balance. The toxicology program is part of the Marine Science Institute, one of 10 Organized Research Units at the Santa Barbara campus. *Photographer: Andy Levin*

LEFT: It could be Christmas morning in Middletown, U.S.A., as Steve Ritter and Idris Hsi play with toy trains in the Distributed Cognition Laboratory at UC San Diego. But there's no time for fun and games as the pair participates in a study of how teams function in the workplace. Each of them controls part, but not all, of the trains' capacities of speed, direction and the coupling and uncoupling of cars. By sharing what they know with each other—and with a third student, who sits in another room and monitors the trains' progress on a computer screen—they try to make the trains run in a coordinated manner. Approximately 200 UCSD undergrads major in cognitive science, which includes the study of the interactions between the human mind and its environment, as well as human, animal and artificial intelligence. *Photographer: Rick Rickman*

BELOW LEFT: Just over the hill from the internationally renowned Silicon Valley, Santa Cruz students Dorian LeCroy and Daniel Kimble try to figure out the next step in their microprocessor laboratory class project. *Photographer: Jim Gensheimer*

RIGHT: In front of a machine known as a nano-engineering multilayer synthesis apparatus, Lawrence Livermore materials scientist Troy Barbee shows off his latest invention: a copper-and-zirconium disk about 1/500th of an inch thick and made up of 2,500 layers of material. The atomically engineered thin multilayer materials are much stronger than conventional alloys, and they hold the promise of improving performance in applications as diverse as integrated circuits and extremely low-temperature, or cryogenic, refrigerators. "It's really exciting," says Barbee, one of about 8,000 employees of the Lab, "to be sitting there looking at something and knowing that it exists nowhere else in the world." *Photographer: Mark Richards*

ABOVE AND RIGHT: It's a bird, it's a plane, it's . . . a senior project! Graduating seniors in Irvine's Department of Mechanical and Aerospace Engineering are required to conceive and construct a group design project and to present it to a crowd gathered in Engineering Plaza on Senior Design Display Day a few days before graduation. At right, Lynne Low and Sean Okamoto look on as their partner Chuck Wang demonstrates the Indy-style race car they built with two other students. The project wasn't quite finished in time: "We bit off more than we could chew," says Okamoto, "even though we worked 10 hours a day on it throughout the year and around-the-clock the last two weeks." Still, Okamoto was pleased: "I've always dreamed," he says, "of building a car."

For Jonn Beeson and Chris San Marchi (*above*), building a helium-filled, remote-controlled blimp was as much an exercise in human relations as in mechanical engineering. "Getting seven people to agree on a design and then find a mutually agreeable time for construction was difficult," Beeson says. That's precisely the point, according to associate professor Michael McCarthy: "The senior project challenges students in everything," he says, "from engineering and manufacturing to salesmanship and management." *Photographer: Rick Rickman*

Left: Three glass domes crown the Hearst Memorial Mining Building, the three-story Berkeley monument built by Phoebe Apperson Hearst in 1896 as a memorial to her late husband George—one of many out-of-staters to embrace the California dream and strike it big during the frenzied years of the Gold Rush. The building still provides a locale for classes in mining, geology and petroleum engineering and is one of four locales on the Cal campus to bear the Hearst name. Mrs. Hearst, UC's first woman regent and the mother of newspaper magnate William Randolph Hearst, contributed some $1.5 million to the university—about $15 million in 1992 dollars. *Photographer: Chris Maynard*

Above: "I study in weird positions sometimes," says chemical engineering major Mareia Frost, "so I don't get cramped in one position." Frost staked out a carrel at Berkeley's Moffitt Undergraduate Library to review her notes for a chemistry exam, despite her misgivings about being able to concentrate at Moffitt: "It's such a big place," she says, "and around exam time there's a lot of noise from the rustling of papers." Library officials say Moffitt receives nearly a million visits a year; the number was even higher before 1991, when the university restricted the general public's access to the library. *Photographer: Jim Gensheimer*

Overleaf: It's a starry, starry night in the hills east of San Jose, where astronomers from throughout the UC system come to use the telescopes at Mount Hamilton's Lick Observatory. The observatory, now administered by UC Santa Cruz, was established in 1888. *Photographer: Jim Gensheimer*

IN SEARCH OF THE UNEXPECTED

Berkeley

Davis

Irvine

Los Angeles

Riverside

San Diego

San Francisco

Santa Barbara

Santa Cruz

It was on Thursday morning, April 23, 1992, that Dr. George Smoot of the Lawrence Berkeley Laboratory made his fabulous announcement on behalf of the Cosmic Background Explorer group (COBE). Later in the day he would say, "If you're religious, it's like looking at God." Frankly, Dr. Smoot's announcement appeared as a dim star in a black sky of news those last days of April in California—news which included an execution, a series of earthquakes and the rioting in Los Angeles. Few among the public were immediately aware of what had happened to our understanding of the universe. One wonders at what depth the news will finally settle, and how the increasing disparity between those rich and poor in scientific knowledge will affect policymaking in the next century.

But who among astronomers and physicists on that Thursday could have cared? In their small offices all over the world, where the view out the window sometimes seems less real, even less beautiful, than the view on the computer terminal, this was an epiphany day.

"This is as fundamentally important," Dr. Grant Matthews, an astrophysicist at Lawrence Livermore, explained some weeks later, "as when Copernicus realized the earth is not the center of the universe. We have a whole fullness of understanding that we didn't have before."

What we have now is proof of the Big Bang, that mysterious moment when a universeful of matter and light was flung out like a parachute catching the wind, expanding in every direction—from every direction—at the speed of light. As a theory, the Big Bang has been taken seriously for 25 years, and scientists have constructed many computer models describing it. But not until just now has the theory been proven by observation.

The description of this revelation belies its significance: Using a satellite orbiting 550 miles above the earth on a trajectory passing over both poles, scientists were able to detect density fluctuations in the afterglow of radiation from the Big Bang itself. In effect, these fluctuations are clumps of light, the seeds from which came stars and planets—and life.

What came before the Big Bang is among the next targets of investigation. The most widely accepted theory describes something called a "false vacuum." It's also known as the "surface of last scattering," conjuring foreboding images of a cosmic diaspora. It is, or was, a paradoxical and dreamlike region of space-time, a region without matter though not a void—on the contrary, an active medium in which matter and antimatter appear to quiver and fluctuate. Apparently there were natural laws, structure and texture. It was a state of existence in which things were going in and out of being, things were happening. Eventually this region became unstable and decayed. And from a particle smaller than an atom came an enormous release of energy—the Big Bang.

Aside from knowledge of the universe, the COBE find also provides insight into the organic nature of theories and models. Before the discovery, there were some 94 models of the Big Bang; now only about 20 still hold. Others are being revised. On the very day of the announcement, in fact, one scientist who was going to offer a theory on what would be revealed by COBE withdrew his presentation, committing "intellectual hara-kiri," as one colleague put it.

It is the theories, of course, that make the boundaries of knowledge billow out—much like the universe itself. It's a funny thing about theories: the larger and more complicated they are, the more minute are the natural phenomena they seek to explain. Moreover, each new theory spins off other theorems as it expands, as well as proofs of what were merely possibilities in previous stages. There is a continual process of evolution by which a simple theorem becomes increasingly complex.

LEFT: A guardian of wisdom helps hold up an arch above the main entrance to the Powell Library at UCLA. The collections of the various libraries in the UC system total more than 20 million volumes, many of which can be located easily through a computer search network. *Photographer: Jim Mendenhall*

"What I've noticed," says Dr. Matthews, "is that when theories become too complex, when you start adding things to the theory to get it to explain what it cannot explain, it becomes baroque. It becomes ornamental. And at that point you often begin to see the underlying problems. Then what inevitably happens is that someone comes along with a simpler theory that knocks off some of the ornaments."

It appears there are always limits to the breadth and depth a theory may offer. Einstein's was not able to unify concepts of gravitational and electromagnetic forces. The Grand Unified Theory of Everything did that by acknowledging the existence of other, previously undefined forces, including the so-called "strong" and "weak" forces. But that theory could not show how to "quantize" gravity to put it on the same footing as the other forces. Along came string theory, which explained the relationship between these different forces by resolving seeming contradictions in the nature of time. Yet that solution in turn left another problem: a string theory's predictions cannot be tested experientially. The theory's beauty—and its flaw—is that it is so abstract.

All of which is to say that despite the COBE results, and despite very powerful theories and proofs, we may never know exactly what happened in those microseconds before and after the Big Bang. We cannot explain the natural laws that apply over such an infinitesimal period of time—a period in seconds of between 10^{-9}, a billionth, and 10^{-44}, an amount so esoteric it can barely be imagined except by letters and numbers on a blackboard.

The theory that theories have their limits, and that there is always a theory that cannot be proven, was first formally "proved," at least in the worlds of geometry and arithmetic, by a German mathematician named Kurt Gödel. In 1963, Stanford University professor Paul Cohen proved that Gödel's theory also applies to set theory, which implies a much broader truth. That truth, in a slightly different context, may be that we can never prove the existence of order or disorder. We may never know if order is the nature of the universe—regardless of what may appear to be true.

"If you look at the magnetic fields in the galactic center," explains UCLA astronomy professor Mark Morris, who

studies dying stars and black holes, "they *appear* to be chaotic lines running hither and yon. But instead of being a twisted jumble, the magnetic fields, we found, are in fact highly ordered. This discovery was completely unexpected, and a glorious moment for that reason. I think it's true in any area of science where progress is being made that you find order emerging out of chaos."

Or consider the paradox suggested by the Second Law of Thermodynamics, which posits that order is always moving toward disorder, that entropy is always increasing, that everything is heading toward decay. As Dr. Matthews points out, "Increasing entropy is actually an example of order, because entropy guarantees that time is moving in one direction. You can't become young again. There's always that progression. Entropy is one definition of time, which is one element of order."

But does order lead to chaos, or vice versa? Is the universe an orderly system inside a chaotic system or the other way around? Does order have any meaning without disorder? In a theoretical sense, are they distinguishable? Are they actually opposite sides of the same phenomenon? These questions suggest the endless expanse of what an astronomer or an astrophysicist might call the cold dark matter of intellectual life.

D r. Minh Duong-van is a physicist at Lawrence Livermore National Laboratory. He was one of the first Vietnamese to receive a Ph.D. in high-energy physics in the United States, and he has become a prominent authority on chaos theory. Chaos has drawn increasing attention in the last fifteen years since the "Santa Cruzians," as they were called, or the Chaos Cabal, first began tinkering with the idea that many aspects of nature are intrinsically unpredictable. Chaos theory has implications for research in artificial intelligence, astronomy, physics and most of the other sciences. But it also has implications for a revised understanding of the logic of scientific thought itself.

Minh Duong-van believes that whether it's a thermal convection system heated to a chaotic state—such as might be found in a weather system—or looters during a riot, inherent feedback systems are always present that act to control chaos. He believes that order can be restored out of chaos given the proper feedback, and he has just finished developing theoretical models that describe the control of chaos in lasers.

Dr. Duong-van has extended his equations to suggest a truth about the nature not only of order and disorder, but of truth itself. He took a pencil, drew a line down the middle of a yellow notebook pad, and wrote "True" on one side, "False" on the other. "I put my pencil on the line. I ask myself, is the point on the left or the right? At this scale, it looks like it's on the line, but given a finer point and a thinner line it's harder to tell because the line is not really straight. It's erratic. You can look still more closely, but at each scale it is the same. Theoretically, if you took an infinitely sharp pencil and tried to find a point on either side of the line, you might find it. But this is where the vacuum comes along. In the real world, with the vacuum, the line is always moving. There is no way to find a point on one side of the line or the other. I cannot prove whether I am on True or False.

"This is what chaos theory says, that there is no straight line. The erratic fluctuations are fractals. In my unorthodox view, we are taught that it is okay if we cannot find the line between true and false. There are some phenomena about which we cannot decide. This is in keeping with Gödel and Cohen—that we cannot prove all theorems. We can spend a lifetime trying to find the line, to know, but we may not know. It is simply beyond us. Of course we try to find the answer anyway. It is our nature to try. We try each theory to see if that explains this phenomenon, and there is an infinite number of theorems to try, but we know there will always

be one that is beyond us. To a scientist, this is reassuring—that even with all the knowledge we have, and will have, we are still allowed not to know everything. And once you understand what this limitation means—this is consciousness, awareness. If you like, this is in the region of God, Buddha. Whatever you believe."

And what of morality, in this world of vacuums where the line between true and false cannot be determined? Duong-van shook his head. "It is our illusion," he insisted. "As a scientist, I cannot find that. It is like a theorem we cannot prove. We are not familiar with that, we cannot determine it. So there is no use trying to understand that right now."

Duong-van believes that physical science and philosophy come together at a point he calls the "right moment." It's a fractal, if you will, a synchronic instant, fate, a completely existential moment of free choice. The consequences of the right choice for a particular person form a kind of feedback, which in turn leads him or her down the appropriate Karmic path. To be sure, Duong-van's notion is highly cerebral; but for those who occupy the realm of scientific abstraction on a day-to-day basis, such ideas can be crucial in reconciling the disciplines of the mind with the longings of the soul.

At the opposite end of the science world from Duong-van lies the domain of Dr. Keith Holyoak, a psychology professor at UCLA. He studies cognitive thinking and symbolic connectionism in relation to artificial intelligence. His work has an interesting implication in the study of order and disorder.

Scientists are discovering that we think along two tracks. One is linear and logical. The other is intuitive, formless, and based on associations. "Rutherford described the atom as like the solar system," says Dr. Holyoak. "On the surface, there would appear to be no relationship, in terms of scale or the forces at work. But in terms of basic relationships, there's a match. It reflects an intuitive understanding. Thinking in terms of analogies and metaphors may be a sign of an instinctual ability that is every bit as important in solving problems, and also simply as a way of thinking. ... What we're finding is that an expert is someone capable of doing something at the 'right time.'"

The notion of the "right time," the right moment, echoes throughout academe these days. In one way or another, directly or indirectly, a great deal of scientific research is devoted to learning what the right moment is and how it comes about. Whether the Big Bang, or the microseconds afterward, or the time when an electron is most likely to be near a certain position relative to the nucleus of an atom, the right moment seems to occur in that no-man's land between order and chaos. It's the same moment as when the poet finds the right word, when the home-run hitter finds the ball—when one person finally trusts another. It is the moment when one knows, beyond any doubt, that something in the universe has revealed itself.

ABOVE: Neanderthal and Australopithecus busts await a student's attention in a back room at Berkeley's Museum of Paleontology. *Photographer: Andy Levin*

RIGHT: Nine million years after *Gomphotherium simpsoni*, a small species of mastodon, roamed the wilds of northern California, a fiberglass cast of a surviving skeleton gets an elevator ride at the Museum of Paleontology, where staff member Mike Tiffany is readying the model for the drive to suburban Danville and temporary installation at the UC Museum at Blackhawk. The 200-pound cast, assembled by museum scientist Mark Goodwin from bones found on the slopes of Mount Diablo, is one of the hundreds of thousands of well-cataloged specimens and displays that have made the Museum of Paleontology a vital resource for UC students, as well as for scientists and researchers around the world who examine museum materials both on site and through loans. The museum, which is also open to the public, boasts the largest fossil collection in the western United States. *Photographer: Andy Levin*

ABOVE: Doctoral student Pamela Chu adjusts a meter on a crossed-molecular-beam machine in Berkeley's Giauque Hall, where she works with chemistry professor and Nobel laureate Yuan Lee. The study of crossed molecular beams helps Lee and his students deepen their understanding of atomic and molecular processes, including the energy transfer between molecules. Lee's work won the Nobel prize in 1986, and he is now one of 11 Nobel laureates on the Berkeley campus. The Associated Research Councils rates Berkeley's graduate departments in chemistry, physics and mathematics as the best in the country, a ranking due in part to students' hard work: Pamela Chu says she puts in about 70 hours a week in Lee's lab, because "it's fun and interesting."
Photographer: Doug Menuez

RIGHT: Student Lisa Plato examines a priceless *cartonnage*—the outer covering of an Egyptian mummy—in the storage area at the Phoebe Apperson Hearst Museum at Berkeley, formerly known as the Lowie Museum. The museum, founded in 1901, was the beneficiary of many turn-of-the-century expeditions to Egypt, Peru, the Mediterranean and Central America. It now houses more than 650,000 cataloged items, with an internationally renowned collection of pre-dynastic Egyptian objects and noteworthy collections from the civilizations of ancient Peru and the Mediterranean. Many of the museum's holdings are nearly 5,000 years old. *Photographer: Chris Maynard*

ABOVE: Backyard scientist Donald Cram, the winner of the 1987 Nobel prize in chemistry, shows off the tools of the trade he has plied at UCLA since 1947. Although he occasionally uses computer-generated modeling programs at his office on campus, Cram often relies on old-fashioned models when working on the back porch of his home in Bel Air. To hear him tell it, the key to his work is simple: "I work on taking what is implicit," he says, "and making it explicit." *Photographer: Mark Wexler*

LEFT: A man at home in his castle, physicist Jay Marx monitors progress on the construction of the Advanced Light Source facility at Lawrence Berkeley Laboratory. When completed, the two-acre ALS will be capable of producing X-ray and ultraviolet light 100 times brighter than existing sources anywhere in the world and will be a boon to materials scientists, chemists, biologists and engineers alike. Chemists, for instance, might track chemical reactions usually measured in trillionths of a second, while biologists hope to produce 3-D holograms of the structures deep within living cells. The ALS project is being built on the site where LBL founder Ernest Lawrence constructed a 184-inch cyclotron in 1938, and the new structure retains the dome of the original Cyclotron building. Lawrence Berkeley, first established in 1931 as the UC Radiation Lab, is the oldest of the country's nine national laboratories and coordinates research projects in a variety of scientific fields. *Photographer: Doug Menuez*

LEFT: Scientists and technicians make adjustments to Alexis, an X-ray imaging satellite built at Los Alamos National Laboratory in New Mexico. The satellite, powered by solar panels, features six telescopes, each about the size of a coffee can; it was developed to scan the entire sky every six months, transmitting back to Los Alamos information about soft, or low-energy, X-ray emissions from a variety of celestial bodies. Los Alamos, created in 1943 to design and build the world's first nuclear weapon under the direction of UC Berkeley physicist J. Robert Oppenheimer, has been managed by the University of California since its inception. *Photographer: P.F. Bentley*

BELOW LEFT: David Hilyard, chief optician of the Lick Observatory, measures the curve of an optical secondary mirror for the telescope at the W.M. Keck Observatory in Hawaii, a joint project of UC and the California Institute of Technology. The world's largest and most powerful telescope, it owes its strength to a system of computer-controlled mirrors. This mirror, polished for three years on the Santa Cruz campus, required a surface so smooth that the tallest blemish could be no higher than 1.5 millionths of an inch. *Photographer: Jim Gensheimer*

RIGHT: The astronomer's mecca sits high upon a Hawaiian mountaintop: It's the Keck Observatory, here under construction. The telescope's system of computer-controlled mirrors consists of 36 thin hexagonal segments, each six feet across, that give researchers the power to observe astronomical phenomena 12 or 13 billion light-years away from earth. By gazing far into the universe, UC astronomers hope to answer questions that have puzzled humankind from time immemorial. "How did we get here?" asks UCSC astronomer Sandra Faber. "Are we unique in the universe? These telescopes will give us a chance to find out." *Photographer: Serge Brunier/Ciel et Espace*

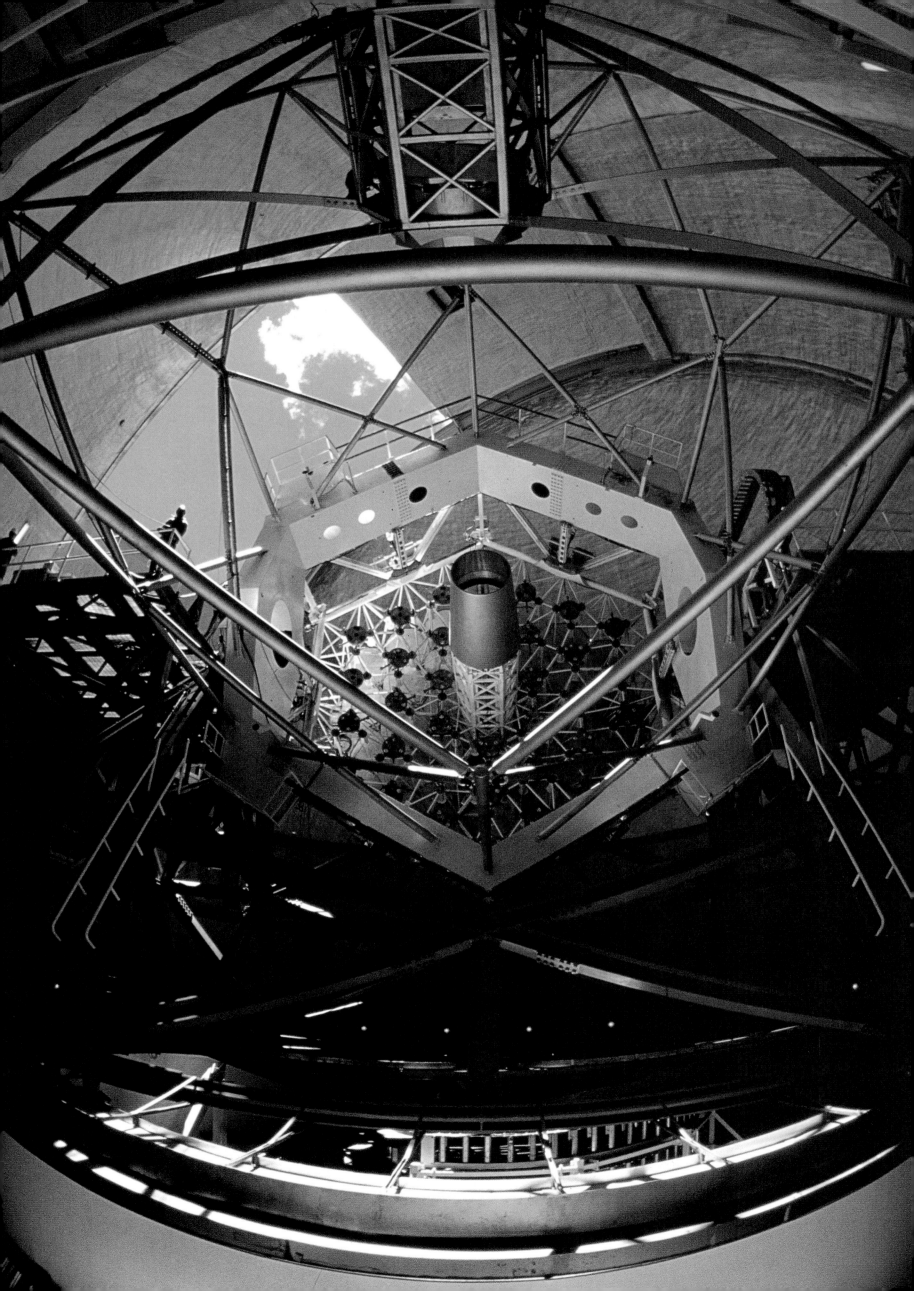

PRECEDING PAGE: Shauna Kubose reads George Orwell's classic novel *1984* in the comfort of her Santa Cruz dorm room. The room Kubose shares with her friend Wendy Gee is a far cry from those of earlier generations: The two women cook meals with a microwave oven and make use of a telephone, a television, a Nintendo set and a refrigerator as well. While the creature comforts stamp her as a student of the '90s, Gee's favorite part of dorm life is one that independent-minded college students have voiced throughout the history of higher education: "The best part of living in the dorms," she says, "is not living with my family." *Photographer: Jim Gensheimer*

NO FREAKING OUT!!

LEFT: It's finals time for students in Human Parasitology at Irvine. Half of each student's course grade will be determined by the test, which consists of 100 fill-in-the-blank questions about tropical diseases such as malaria and sleeping sickness. The maladies that affect students around exam time are less dramatic than malaria, but counselors and doctors worry nonetheless about the health of cramming students, who are likely to increase their caffeine intake, cut down on sleep and exercise, take both prescription and nonprescription drugs, and alter their already irregular eating habits.
Photographer: Jim Mendenhall

TOP: Good advice at Santa Cruz or any university campus, especially during exams.
Photographer: Jim Gensheimer

ABOVE: A student at Irvine racks his brain in an effort to remember the mosquito genus and species responsible for the transmission of yellow fever. As survivors of Stuart Krassner's Human Parasitology course know, the best answer is *Aëdes aegypti.*
Photographer: Jim Mendenhall

PRECEDING PAGE: Rush hour at UC San Diego.
Photographer: Dana Fineman

ABOVE AND RIGHT: It's the end of the school year at UCLA—time to move panda bears, tennis shoes and other prized possessions out of the dorm and to beg your father to help vacuum your room. About three-quarters of the first-year students live on campus at UCLA. Other students commute from their parents' homes; rent apartments in or around the campus in the Westwood district of Los Angeles; or live in fraternities, sororities or house-like residence halls known as cooperatives.
Photographer: Jim Mendenhall

OVERLEAF: College is a kick for a group of Riverside students, who flash their soccer skills against the backdrop of the San Bernardino Mountains.
Photographer: Andy Levin

"The facilities here are good," says Mark McAdam, one of about 700 disabled students at Berkeley. "I can get around by myself most of the day." The Disabled Students' Program, which resulted in part from the Berkeley-based Independent Living Movement in the early 1970s, helps disabled students lead independent lives by offering help with admissions, enrollment and housing, as well as wheelchair repair and attendant referral. "Most professors take everything into consideration," adds McAdam, a chemistry major who has set his sights on graduate school. "They have to, because there's such a big disabled community here."
Photographer: Andy Levin

ABOVE, LEFT: While Mitch Sanders catches up on the week's news, Brian Quigley, Michelle Van Sambeek, Shawn Stepper and Greg Placer work on getting dinner ready in Van Sambeek's on-campus apartment at UC San Diego. "Last year," says Van Sambeek, "we all lived in the dorm together, so this year we try to get together for dinner every once in a while." It's a wonder Van Sambeek has the time to host dinner parties: Besides carrying a full load of sociology classes, she tutors for three hours a week in a San Diego elementary school and directs a campus group called Volunteer Connection, which matches up UCSD students with community agencies that need volunteers. *Photographer: Dana Fineman*

ABOVE: Pizza chef Michael Woodward serves up his latest creation at Sluggo's, the cooperatively run restaurant at UC Santa Cruz's Porter College. About half of Santa Cruz's students work in addition to taking classes, but not all of them find the same satisfaction as Woodward: "What is the sound of one pizza spinning?" he asks. He then offers his own answer: It is "the molding of mind, body and soul into the rotating dough." *Photographer: Jim Gensheimer*

LEFT: If a Berkeley student knows only two words of Italian, it's a safe bet they're *espresso* and *cappuccino*. Coffee houses such as the Bancroft Cafe, where C.J. Rendic, standing, and Rhonda Lesinski have come to study for finals, line the streets on both the north and south side of campus. Some have become bona fide cultural monuments: The poet Allen Ginsberg is said to have written parts of his beatnik anthem *Howl* (with its reference to "Angel-headed hipsters ... who passed through universities with radiant cool eyes hallucinating Arkansas and Blake-light tragedy among the scholars of war") in Telegraph Avenue's Cafe Med. *Photographer: Jim Gensheimer*

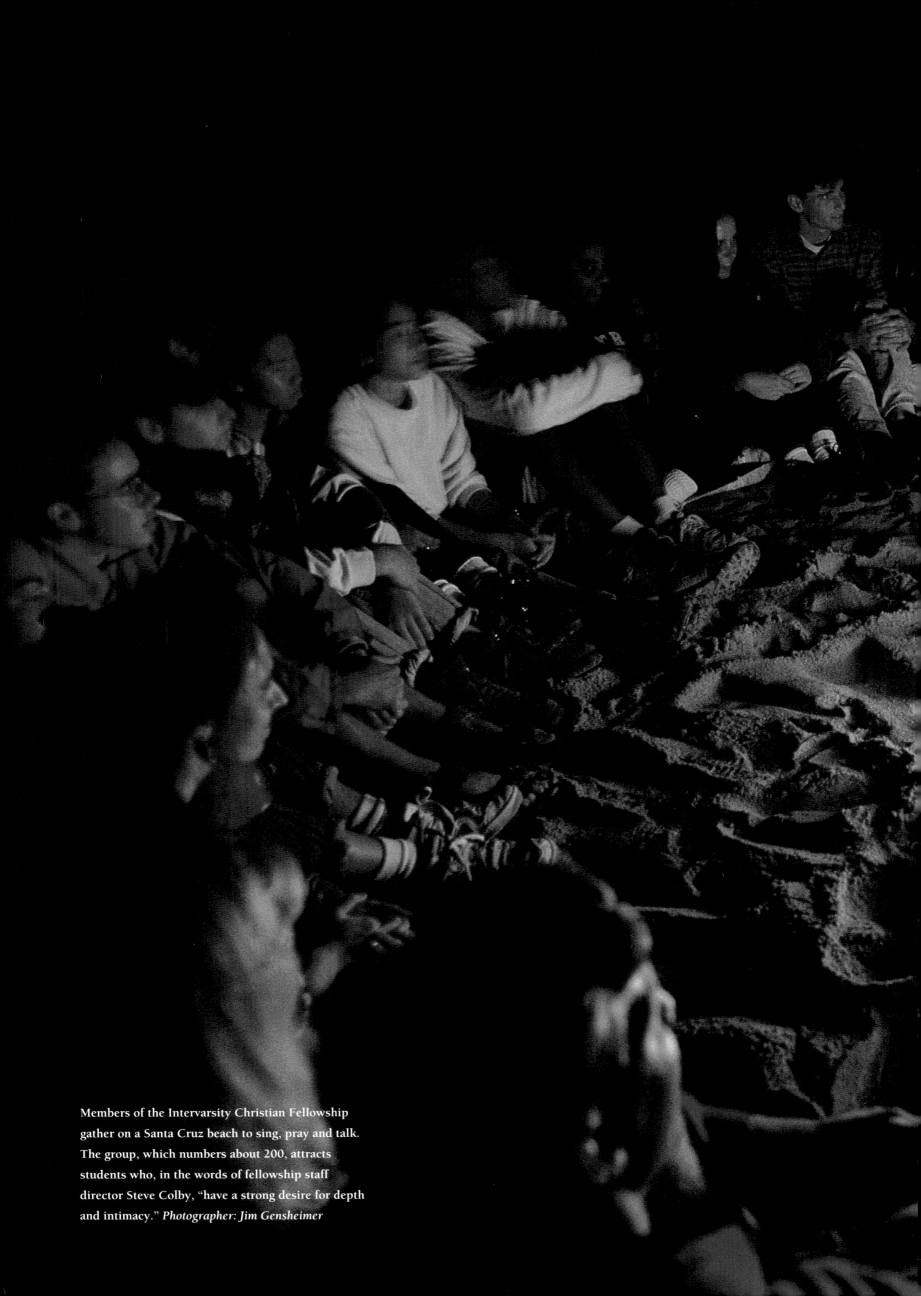

Members of the Intervarsity Christian Fellowship
gather on a Santa Cruz beach to sing, pray and talk.
The group, which numbers about 200, attracts
students who, in the words of fellowship staff
director Steve Colby, "have a strong desire for depth
and intimacy." *Photographer: Jim Gensheimer*

TOP: Adrian Kragen, professor emeritus of Berkeley's School of Law at Boalt Hall, gets a touchup from Julie Layne of the Office of Public Ceremonies before joining his faculty colleagues for their entry into the Hearst Greek Theater for the annual Berkeley Convocation. The color of Kragen's robe gives him away as a Cal graduate: class of 1931, Boalt class of 1934. He taught tax law at his alma mater from 1952 to 1991 and now says, "I have great affection for Berkeley. I like the students, and the faculty is both congenial and able." Besides Berkeley, there are law schools at UC Davis, UCLA and in San Francisco at the UC-affiliated Hastings College of the Law. *Photographer: Chris Maynard*

ABOVE: A graduating senior at UC San Diego puts his best foot forward as he strides up to collect his diploma. *Photographer: Rick Rickman*

BELOW: "I carried her most of the school year," says Katherine Rodriguez of her daughter, Cassandra, "so I wanted her with me when I got my diploma." Here, husband Richard hands the five-week-old infant to Katherine just before degrees are conferred at graduation ceremonies at UC San Diego's Muir College. "Graduation was an unbelievable day," says Rodriguez. "I was ecstatic, but also a bit numb."

Soon after receiving her diploma, Rodriguez was at work teaching sixth grade in a Spanish-English bilingual classroom at Emery Park School in the Los Angeles suburb of Alhambra. "I miss UC San Diego," she says—"the school, the fellowship, the people. The liberal arts education at UCSD prepares you for anything. It prepares you for life."

Photographer: Rick Rickman

ABOVE: In a scene that California Governor Henry Haight could scarcely have imagined when he signed a bill authorizing the establishment of the university in 1868, graduates at Santa Cruz celebrate one of the biggest days of their lives.
Photographer: Jim Gensheimer

RIGHT: About 38,000 students received undergraduate and graduate degrees from the university in 1991; the first UC graduates in 1873, who attended classes in Oakland until the first two buildings were completed on the Berkeley campus, numbered 12. Then as now, forward-looking graduates embodied the expansive words of Bishop George Berkeley, the 18th-century Irish philosopher and educator after whom the city of Berkeley was named: "Westward the course of empire takes its way!" *Photographer: Rick Rickman*

○ **NATURAL RESERVES**

BERKELEY
1) Chickering American River Reserve, Placer County (1,699 acres)
2) Hastings Natural History Reservation, Monterey County (2,002 acres)
3) Northern California Coast Range Preserve, Mendocino County (7,520 acres)
4) Pygmy Forest Reserve, Mendocino County (70 acres)

DAVIS
5) Bodega Bay Marine Reserve, Sonoma County (416 acres)
6) Eagle Lake Field Station, Lassen County (62 acres)
7) Jepson Prairie Reserve, Solano County (1,566 acres)
8) Stebbins Cold Canyon Reserve, Solano and Napa counties (579 acres)
9) Quail Ridge Ecological Reserve, Napa County (1,700 acres)

IRVINE
10) Burns Piñon Ridge Reserve, San Bernardino County (265 acres)
11) San Joaquin Freshwater Marsh Reserve, Orange County (202 acres)

LOS ANGELES
12) Santa Monica Mountains Reserve, Los Angeles County (760 acres)

RIVERSIDE
13) Box Springs Reserve, Riverside County (160 acres)
14) Phillip L. Boyd Deep Canyon Desert Research Center, Riverside County (16,700 acres)
15) Emerson Wildlife Preserve, Riverside County (185 acres)
16) Granite Mountains Reserve, San Bernardino County (8,920 acres)
17) James San Jacinto Mountains Reserve, Riverside County (29 acres)
18) Motte Rimrock Reserve, Riverside County (472 acres)
19) Sacramento Mountains Reserve, San Bernardino County (591 acres)

SAN DIEGO
20) Dawson Los Monos Canyon Reserve, San Diego County (163 acres)
21) Elliot Chaparral Reserve, San Diego County (107 acres)
22) Kendall-Frost Mission Bay Marsh Reserve, San Diego County (16 acres)
23) Scripps Coastal Reserve, San Diego County (943 acres)

SANTA BARBARA
24) Carpinteria Salt Marsh Reserve, Santa Barbara County (120 acres)
25) Coal Oil Point Reserve, Santa Barbara County (117 acres)
26) Fish Slough Area of Critical Environmental Concern, Mono County (36,000 acres)
27) Santa Cruz Island Reserve, Santa Barbara County (54,488 acres)
28) Valentine Eastern Sierra Reserve, Mono County (187 acres)

SANTA CRUZ
29) Año Nuevo Island Reserve, San Mateo County (8 acres)
30) Landels-Hill Big Creek Reserve, Monterey County (3,848 acres)
31) Younger Lagoon Reserve, Santa Cruz County (26 acres)

DAVIS
Opened 1959
Acres 5,200
Enrollment 23,302
Employees 19,819

SAN FRANCISCO
Opened 1873
Acres 107
Enrollment 3,756
Employees 12,752

BERKELEY
Opened 1873
Acres 1,232
Enrollment 30,372
Employees 17,896

SANTA CRUZ
Opened 1965
Acres 2,000
Enrollment 10,136
Employees 4,746

● **AGRICULTURAL AND NATURAL RESOURCE RESEARCH AND EXTENSION CENTERS**

(A) Tulelake Center, Siskiyou County
(B) Sierra Foothill Center, Yuba County
(C) Hopland Center, Mendocino County
(D) Deciduous Fruit Research Station, Santa Clara County
(E) Kearney Agricultural Research Field Station, Fresno County
(F) Lindcove Center, Tulare County
(G) West Side Center, Fresno County
(H) South Coast Center, Orange County
(I) Imperial Valley Center, Imperial County

▢ **DEPARTMENT OF ENERGY LABORATORIES**

(1) LAWRENCE BERKELEY LABORATORY
Opened 1931
Employees 3,000

(2) LAWRENCE LIVERMORE NATIONAL LABORATORY
Opened 1952
Employees 7,800

(3) LOS ALAMOS, NEW MEXICO NATIONAL LABORATORY
Opened 1943
Employees 6,800

LOS ANGELES
Opened 1919
Acres 419
Enrollment 36,366
Employees 20,280

RIVERSIDE
Opened 1954
Acres 1,200
Enrollment 8,890
Employees 3,100

SANTA BARBARA
Opened 1958
Acres 815
Enrollment 18,519
Employees 4,396

IRVINE
Opened 1965
Acres 1,522
Enrollment 16,950
Employees 8,842

SAN DIEGO
Opened 1959
Acres 2,040
Enrollment 17,958
Employees 17,220

PROJECT PHOTOGRAPHERS

P.F. Bentley
Stinson Beach, California
Bentley is a *Time* magazine photographer whose past assignments have included election coverage in El Salvador and Panama. His awards include first-place honors in the National Press Photographers Association Pictures of the Year competition in 1984 and 1988 for his coverage of the U.S. presidential campaigns.

Ricardo DeAratanha
Los Angeles, California
DeAratanha began his career with the *Jornal do Brasil* and is a three-time winner in the Nikon Photo Contest International. He is a member of the Image Bank. His work has appeared in numerous Brazilian and American publications, including several Collins books. He currently works for the *Los Angeles Times*.

Dana Fineman
Los Angeles, California
A member of the Sygma photo agency, Fineman studied at the Art Center College of Design in Pasadena, California. Her work appears regularly in *New York*, *People*, *Time*, *Newsweek* and *Stern*.

Jim Gensheimer
San Jose, California
A native of Louisville, Kentucky, Gensheimer worked for two years for the *Louisville Courier-Journal* and now shoots for the *San Jose Mercury News*. His awards include a 1982 prize in the William Randolph Hearst Foundation Photojournalism Championship, a Photographer of the Year Award from the Atlanta Seminar on Photojournalism in 1984 and California Photographer of the Year in 1988.

Annie Griffiths Belt
Silver Spring, Maryland
Griffiths Belt began assignment work for *National Geographic* in 1978 and has since worked on more than two dozen magazine and book projects. Her photographs have appeared in *Smithsonian*, *Newsweek*, *GEO*, *American Photo*, *Merian* and *Stern*, and she has exhibited in New York, Washington, Moscow and Tokyo. She has received awards from the National Press Photographers Association, the Associated Press, the National Organization for Women and the White House News Photographers Association.

Andy Levin
New York, New York
Levin has covered a wide variety of subjects for news and feature magazines, ranging from AIDS doctors to a nun who operates a clinic for the poor in rural Mississippi. In 1985, Levin received top honors in the National Press Photographers Association Pictures of the Year competition for his essay on a Nebraska farm family. In 1986, his essay on the Statue of Liberty won similar honors. He works on a freelance basis for clients nationwide.

Marcia Lippman
New York, New York
Lippman, a native New Yorker, divides her time between teaching, freelancing as a commercial photographer and working as an artist. Her clients include *Esquire*, *Interview* and the *New York Times*. In 1987, she won a New York Foundation for the Arts Fellowship in Photography, as well as a commission from the foundation and the New York Metropolitan Transportation Authority to shoot a black-and-white study of the reconstruction of the New York City subways.

Chris Maynard
San Francisco, California
Maynard has been a freelance photographer for 20 years. His editorial and corporate clients include the *New York Times*, *Time*, *Business Week*, IBM and Dun & Bradstreet. He is the co-author of two cookbooks, *Manifold Destiny* and *The Bad For You Cookbook*. He previously worked on Collins' *Baseball in America*.

Jim Mendenhall
Los Angeles, California
Mendenhall's work has appeared in more than 70 magazines, including *Life*, *National Geographic*, *Sports Illustrated*, *Newsweek*, *Forbes* and *GQ*. In 1984, while working for the *Orange County Register*, he was part of a team that won a Pulitzer Prize for its coverage of the Olympics. He currently works as a staff photographer at the *Los Angeles Times*.

Doug Menuez
Mill Valley, California
Formerly with *USA Today*, Menuez now works on assignment around the world for *Time*, *Newsweek*, *U.S. News and World Report*, *Fortune* and other news magazines. In 1987 he founded Reportage, a full-service corporate photojournalism agency specializing in the design and production of annual reports, brochures and photo essays. In 1989, Menuez co-produced *15 Seconds: The Great California Earthquake of 1989*, a book project that sold 70,000 copies and raised $500,000 for earthquake relief.

Chuck O'Rear
St. Helena, California
O'Rear has been a contributing photographer for *National Geographic* for more than 20 years. From his home in California's Napa Valley, he has produced books on both the nearby Silicon Valley and on local vineyards; the latter, entitled *Napa Valley*, was published by Collins Publishers in 1990.

Rick Rickman
Laguna Niguel, California
During the five years he worked for the *Des Moines Register*, Rickman was named Iowa Photographer of the Year three times. In 1985 he won a Pulitzer Prize in Spot News Photography for the *Orange County Register* for coverage of the 1984 Olympics and was chosen California Photographer of the Year. One of his works from *A Day in the Life of China* was featured on the cover of *Time* magazine.

James A. Sugar
Mill Valley, California
Sugar has been a contract photographer for *National Geographic* for 22 years. His corporate clients include IBM, Citibank, AT&T, BP Oil, DuPont and *Flying*. He has been named Magazine Photographer of the Year (and runner-up) by the National Press Photographers Association and has won numerous individual awards from the NPPA and the White House News Photographers Association. Along with several colleagues, he is currently working on a national lecture series on digital photography co-sponsored by Kodak and Apple Computer.

Mark Wexler
Los Angeles, California
Wexler travels the world as a photographer for a variety of editorial and corporate clients, including *Time*, *Life*, *National Geographic*, *Smithsonian* and *GEO*. He won three World Press Photo Foundation awards for his work on Collins' *A Day in the Life of Japan*.

CONTRIBUTING PHOTOGRAPHERS

Ben Ailes *Berkeley, California*
Serge Brunier *Keck Observatory, Hawaii*
Jack Clark/Comstock *Sacramento, California*
Dominique Dallet *Madrid, Spain*
Eric Hanauer *San Diego, California*
Laurel Hungerford *Laguna Beach, California*
Paul Kennedy *Costa Mesa, California*
Lick Observatory *Mt. Hamilton, California*
Dan Murphy *San Francisco, California*
Roger Ressmeyer *Sag Harbor, New York*
Mark Richards *Sausalito, California*
Barrie Rokeach *Berkeley, California*
Rocky Thies *San Diego, California*

ABOUT THE WRITERS

Mark MacNamara
San Francisco, California
Mark MacNamara has been a freelance journalist and editor for 15 years. Recent works have included a story in *Vanity Fair* about a Florida woman accused of serial murder; a profile of Ram Dass for *West*, the Sunday magazine of the *San Jose Mercury News*; and an article in *Los Angeles* magazine involving a man on California's death row. He has also written extensively for the *San Francisco Chronicle*. In 1990, he became editor of *Sequoia*, a bimonthly news magazine about religion and society.

Bernard Ohanian
Berkeley, California
Ohanian is a 1980 UC Berkeley graduate with a B.A. in linguistics and an award-winning magazine writer whose work has appeared in *Hippocrates*, *Parenting*, the *Washington Post* and the *Los Angeles Times Magazine*, among other publications. He has previously worked for Collins as a writer for *A Day in the Life of Italy* and *Baseball in America* and as senior editor for *A Day in the Life of Ireland*. He was also the editor and caption writer for *The Power to Heal* (Prentice-Hall, 1990).

CREDITS

Sponsorship Director
Cathy Quealy

Managing Editor
Bill Messing

Design Director
Jennifer Barry

Project Editor
Barbara Roether

Director of Photography
Sandra Eisert

ACKNOWLEDGMENTS

Literally hundreds of people contributed to the creation of this book, but a few must receive special mention. Clayton Carlson helped get it all started, shepherding and shaping the concept of the book in its early stages. Bernard Ohanian managed the initial steps in the assignment process and later wrote all the captions for the book with research assistance from Anne Maloney. George Olson edited hundreds of rolls of film. Sara Frankel, with help from copy editor Janice Maloney and proofreaders Sara Bethell and Doreen Kan, whipped the text into shape. Kari Perin developed preliminary layouts, and Cecile Chronister labored endlessly over the typography. Ray Potter helped secure funding. And through it all, Ron Kolb saw to it that the interests of countless individuals at UC would be heard and understood. To all, and to many others who can't be named here, our deepest thanks.

FRIENDS AND ADVISERS

Peter Allen
Robert W. Alspaugh
Michael Alva
Lynn Atwood
Pat Baily
William B. Baker
Sharon Bandy
Herbert E. Barker, Jr.
Ann Barkhaus
Kathy Barton
Gary Berg
Chad Bigony
Linda Bisson
Phaly Bith
Donna Blackmore
Diane Bonanno
Amy Bonetti
Ronald W. Brady
Stephanie Burchfield
John Burgess
Betty Byrne
Eileen Callahan
Joseph Calmes
Byron A. Camp
Olivia Cervantes
Barbara Christian
James Clark
Chuck Colgan
Winifred Cox
George Craig
Donald Cram
Edwin M. Crawford
Tony Crouch
Adrienne Dale
Robert Dallek
Steve Davenport
Angela Davis
Dan Dawson
Philip Delgado
Mark Dellins
Alvin Donner
Tasha Dowdakin
Scott Doyon
Oscar Dystel
Sabrina Eastwood
Robert Fairbanks
Lucy Faulkner
Dr. Gerald Finerman
Harriet Fleischer
Katharine Fong
Jerrold K. Footlick
Susan Foster
Rachel Friedland
Lyn Garling
Seth Geiger
Herbert M. Gordon
Linda Granell
Al Hall
Linda Harmeson
Elihu Harris
Benjamin Hayward
John J. Hayward
Joseph Hayward
Linda Hayward
Roger Hines
Sam Hoffman
Sally Holbrook
Maxine Hong Kingston
Linda Hooper
Mark Hooper
Donna Howard
Rose Hsu
Barbara Hufham
Robert Irion
Mark Jordan

Tony Joseph
Judy Katrel Blantz
Thomas L. Kelly
Denise Klarquist
Michael Kleinman
Don Konestrow
Deborah Land
Chris Lathan
Linn Lee
Tom Lee
Rudi Legname
Arsenio Lopez
Bruce Lundy
Christopher S. Lynch
Karen Mack
Rick Malaspina
Angie Malloy
Henry Mancini
Diane Martin
Jay Marx and family
Rick Maslin
Vivian Mayer
Les McCraw
John M. McCready
James Merz
Steve Morange
Margie Moreno
Frank Norris
Janet Norton
Mary Lou Olszewski
Joe Pastrone
Daniel E. Perlman
Karin Peters
Nad Peterson
Wallace Ravven
Michela Reichman
Steve Renick
Amy Rennert
Maril Revette Stratton
Ron Rhody
Jenny Rodriguez
Katherine Rodriguez and family
Jerome Rothenberg
Sherwood Rowland
Susan Rumsey
Delia Salvi
Robert Sanders
Junichi Semitsu and family
Susan Shea
David Simler
John Sims
Sylvia Sleight
Thomas W. Snow
Gary Soto
Geoffrey Stier
Maril Stratton
Carole Swartz
Edward Teller
Kathy Tiano
Mary Tokita
Neil Topham
Arthur Tressler
Alice Trinkel
Alan Villandre
Steve Wampler
Joan Ward
Karen Watson
Margaret Weeks
Richard West
Alex Williams
Kim Wilson
Dan Wohlfeiler
Stuart Wolpert
Jerry Wright
Jacques Yeager
Heidi Yorkshire